New Nations and Peoples

India

India

TAYA ZINKIN

with 100 illustrations and 3 maps

New York
WALKER AND COMPANY

To

ELINOR SINCLAIR

for her goodness

Contents

Introduction

INDIA IS BIG, diverse, old, poor and important. She covers an area of 1,138,814 square miles and is the seventh biggest country in the world. She spans in latitude from Gibraltar to within 550 miles of the Equator, and has mountains above 28,000 feet high and land below sea level.

India has the highest mountains in the world, the Himalayan range with forty peaks over 25,000 feet; she also has lands like the rice fields in parts of Kerala, which are so low that the water has to be pumped out before crops can be sown. There are great deserts where it never rains, but at Cherrapunji, in Assam, it rains 450 inches in a matter of a few months whereas in Ladakh, up in the Himalayas, crops have to be grown from melting glaciers. Temperatures vary from extreme cold up in the high mountains to extreme heat down in the plains. Indeed there can be extremes of temperature within minutes, as in the Punjab where the drop or rise in temperature can be as great as 50 degrees Fahrenheit in winter at sunrise and sunset. In the north of India everything is grey for months before the rains; the baked earth cracks and dust hangs over man and beast more persistent even than flies. In the far south everything is green the whole year round and the enemy is humidity.

Dimension itself makes for diversity. India is shaped like a huge triangle 1,500 miles wide from east to west at its Himalayan base, and 2,000 miles deep from north to south. The climate runs from Alpine to tropical, the biggest rivers are hundreds of miles long and several miles wide at some places. The Indo-Gangetic plain, 1,000 miles long and 200 miles wide, is the largest alluvial plain in the world and has one of the highest densities of population.

Human diversity is equally endless. Indians run the whole gamut from mongoloid to semitic, from negroid to negrito races. There are tall Indians, small Indians, dark Indians, light Indians, Indians who only marry their relatives, others who never marry within their family, some who practise polygamy, others who practise polyandry. All of them have one thing in common: through the centuries they have imbibed a certain underlying oneness based upon history, religion and poverty.

Most Indians live in villages. There is as much diversity in village customs and in village layout and houses as in the people themselves. South Indian villages sometimes consist of rows of well-built houses with pagoda roofs – the pagoda shape is believed to have been carried from India to China through Nepal and Tibet by Buddhist monks. North Indian villages usually have flat roofs, often fortified as in the Middle East, and endlessly connected to each other by roof terraces, as in a North African *Qasba*. In most of central India villages are isolated clusters of mud huts covered with thatch; in parts of Orissa the village is surrounded by a stockade to protect it against wild beasts; in Maharashtra and Gujerat many peasants sleep with their cattle under the same roof; in Bengal the cattle have their own sheds but in the Himalayas they occupy the ground floor. Diversity extends to the villages themselves; some are drab, others are very picturesque with their wall frescoes or little fortifications.

Diversity is not confined to the nature of the villages, it extends to the dress of the people. Dress is most important, it helps to place people just as accent does in Britain. There are as many ways of draping the sari as is necessary to identify the wearer. The women of Gujerat drape it over their shoulder from right to left, their Bengali sisters drape it from left to right, but in Maharashtra it is tucked like trousers between the legs while in Madras it is both tucked and wound. Christian women from the Punjab wind it twice round their waist, while Coorgis wear it back to front. The descendants of those who were converted to Catholicism by St Thomas the Apostle wear pleats at the back of their sari instead of in front like everybody else. The way in which the sari is draped is only one part of the difference; texture and colour are very important too. In

Rajasthan women wear thick gathered skirts, in the Punjab they wear trousers and Muslim women almost everywhere hide beneath the burkha which hangs down to the ground from their skull cap like a tent with grilled slits for the eyes. Similarly, men have as many ways of covering their heads, as many shapes to their turbans, as many colours and twists, as is necessary for everybody to know at once who everybody else is. Indeed this insistence on looking different even extends to beards.

Hair styles are also very useful in placing people. Many men in south India shave the front of their head and wear a bun at the back. Outside Madras, buns are usually worn only by women. Some women wear their bun on the nape of the neck, some have buns shaped like the figure eight, some tuck it under the hair, others wear it sideways, others plait their hair in one plait, others in two plaits, others still in hundreds of little plaits like Egyptian queens, others simply let their hair hang loose. What they do with their hair, what they wear, particularly what jewels and ornaments, is, of course, laid down by tradition and makes it easy to identify them; not only what part of India they come from but what caste they belong to.

With such exuberant diversity goes a great deal of contrast. Contrast in India is not confined to cities and villages, to rich and poor, to palaces and hovels, it goes much further. For example, in the middle of the modern city of Bombay one can find side by side an American car (manufactured in India) and a bullock cart (made in the village); within a few miles from the Atomic Energy Reactor at Chembur, aborigines still live in the Stone Age; on the site of modern steel mills women carry mud in baskets on their heads. Thus the Indian kaleidoscope smoothly glides from the prehistoric to the atomic age because India is still rooted in her ancient history.

India has one of the oldest civilizations of the world and an impressive though patchy historical past. She has given to the world one of its two great religions: Hinduism which, together with its reformed version – Buddhism, has influenced half the people of the world. Moreover India has a distinguished artistic, philosophic and mathematical tradition, and a quite unique social structure which is based on caste.

9

Until the Renaissance, India was much more advanced than the West in many ways. The people of the Indus Civilization were the first to build truly planned cities and houses with sanitation. Also during this period Indian chemistry and mathematics were second to none; it was in India that the zero was invented together with the decimal notation known as 'Arabic' because it was brought from India to the West by Arab traders. Indian dyes and textiles were famous all over the world; the great temples and the rich statuary of Hinduism are among the finest in the world while ancient Hindu philosophy compares favourably with that of the ancient Greeks.

However, dimension, diversity and antiquity are nothing compared with the impact India's poverty makes on the visitor.

Statistics of course tell their grim story: it is widely known that the average per capita income in India is ten shillings a week; that millions of Indians are under-nourished and that probably the majority get too little protein and not enough fat. But these are just cold facts on paper. One has to come to India, one has to live there fully to appreciate the meaning of poverty. When the average per capita income is only ten shillings a week, of which over a shilling goes in taxes and there is no welfare state, £250 a year is a middle-class income. To own a tumble-down second-hand motor car is the equivalent of having a Daimler in Britain or a Cadillac in America; to have running water, and/or electricity in one's home is a luxury comparable to having an all air-conditioned house in America or a house fully staffed with domestic servants in Britain. The villager who owns five acres of reasonable land – on which he has to keep his family of four – is a member of the middle class. He is a respected man in his community, he does not see himself as the poor man he would be in the West. If he owns 30 irrigated acres, he is the envy of his fellow villagers and carries the same weight in his village as a retired colonel or a small country squire does in Britain.

India's poverty has not made Indians communist. The educated classes in India have not been driven into totalitarian shortcuts but are determined to make a success of the democratic method; a method much more in keeping with Hindu tradition than compulsion. It is this determination to raise their standard of living the democratic way which makes the 475 million people of India accept willingly sacrifices no Western electorate has ever inflicted upon itself except in times of war. They are willing to suffer today in the hope that their grandchildren will have a better life in the future. It is a determination rare amongst democracies; a determination which entitles Indians to the sympathy and help of all the richer nations.

India is as important to the world today as she has ever been, despite the gruelling poverty which is keeping her down, because it is above all in India that the synthesis of the ideas of the East and the West is taking place. The form this synthesis will take matters both because of India's size and population – one man in six lives in India – and because of India's strategic location in Asia, wedged as she is between the Indian Ocean and communist China. Above all, India's importance in the world stems from the fact that she has a democratic government, and that alone of the newly independent countries which have come into existence since the Second World War, she has an educated middle class sufficiently large to make a success both of democracy and of technological and economic progress.

1 Antiquity

THE EARLY HISTORY OF INDIA is like an old puzzle from which pieces are missing with the result that much of the picture has to be left blank. This is very largely because Hindus are too concerned with the relationship between man and the divine to interest themselves in such mundane matters as history, unless it be related to religion. It is also due to the fact that India was constantly invaded in the north and constantly prey to local wars in the south so that much historical evidence must have been destroyed, especially as buildings were often made of wood and most records were inscribed on palm leaves. Nearly all we know therefore about India's early history comes either from recent archaeological finds or from the occasional diary of ancient travellers like the Greek Megasthenes (c. 300 B.C.), the Chinese Hiuen-Tsang (c. 620 B.C.), or the Venetian Marco Polo (1254–1324). Nevertheless, until the Rajputs of the ninth century and the Muslim conquest of the twelfth century, after which Indian history was recorded by Muslim court historians for the greater glory of their masters, one can briefly divide early Indian history into six periods.

I   *The Indus Valley Civilization, c. 2500 B.C.–1500 B.C.*
Until the 1920s nothing was known of this great urban civilization which dotted the Indian subcontinent from what is now Pakistan to Gujerat. It has been established that in the Punjab, Sind, the Bay of Cambay and the western Punjab, great cities existed dating back to 2500 B.C. They were far in advance in their organization of any

other cities of the period. For example, at Mohenjodaro in Sind, the houses built in fine fired clay were two storeys high, had bath-rooms with running water and modern drains while the streets were built on the New York pattern of the right-angle grid. In addition there were silos and spacious public buildings inside the city which was protected against the outside world by high walls. The seals, statuettes and utensils which have been excavated show a high degree not only of technical but of artistic skill. The people of the Indus Valley Civilization used a script which has not yet been deciphered so that one can only speculate as to their religious practices. But there is reason to believe that they worshipped the Mother Goddess; a goddess who is still worshipped in India today. Nobody knows how or why the Indus Valley Civilization was wiped out; as with the romantic Atlantis, speculation is rife.

II   The Vedic Age, c. 1500 B.C.–1000 B.C.

All that is known of the half millennium which followed the fall of the Indus Valley Civilization comes from the *Vedas*, a collection of sacred hymns attributed to the Aryans who are believed to have come from the north. The *Vedas*, like the *Iliad*, were for a long time passed down by religious bards who had to depend on their memory.

There are four *Vedas*. The first and oldest is the *Rig-Veda*, which has 1,028 highly mystical and symbolic hymns. The poet Rabin-dranath Tagore called the *Rig-Veda*, the 'poetic testament of a people's collective reaction to the wonder and awe of existence'.

The *Vedas* deal with the way in which the people of northeast India lived and thought from about 1500 B.C. Little is known about them except that they owned cattle and were ruled by warriors who depended on priests to perform the ritual which protected crops and cattle and insured victory in war. Victory in war was most important because on the one hand clan wars were endemic, and on the other hand there were enemies: the 'Dasyus', who are called 'black', though this may have been abuse rather than description. Whether the Dasyus were backward aborigines or the highly civilized people of the Indus Valley Civilization is to this day open to speculation.

Until a few years ago, when archaeologists set the seal of authenticity upon legend, the society described in the epics was merely part of Indian mythology; now it has acquired historical roots. There are three great epics, and it is upon them that Hinduism is based. The *Ramayana* and the *Mahabharata* are very reminiscent of the *Iliad* and the *Odyssey*, although they are much more concerned with religious and righteous action and duty. Indeed, the *Bhagavad Gita*, which is a part of the *Mahabharata*, is wholly concerned with religious duty and is to the Hindus what the Bible is to Christians. The third epic, the *Upanishads*, are philosophic discourses illustrated by folk tales.

It is from these epics that one gets a picture of the history of that period. Society was rural and people lived in fortified camps. There were no big cities, which may be the reason why practically nothing of this civilization has remained. The social organization was not very different from that of early Scotland, with its clans and its emancipation of women who were fully part of society. But the resemblance ends there, for the epic society is already divided into four castes which are functional like the European guilds. There are the Brahmins or priests who are responsible for handing down the *Vedas* by word of mouth, for setting an example of rightful living, and helping people with advice. Next come the warriors whose duty is to fight and rule; then the merchants and the artisans and then the peasants. At the bottom of society, outside the four castes, there are the Outcastes whose duty is to perform unclean tasks like scavenging, fishing or handling carrion. And side by side with the Hindus, totally unaffected, the aborigines who probably ruled most of India.

During the Epic Age caste division was still fluid: a Brahmin with a liking for war could become a warrior; a philosophically inclined warrior could become a priest, even an Outcaste could become a priest if he was adopted by a sage; and kings could also marry Outcastes. An example of the latter practice was the mother of the Pandavas, the great heroes of the *Mahabharata*, who was an Outcaste.

The epics have a more important place in India than the Bible has in the West. This is because the behaviour of the epic heroes is still the model for everybody, and even in the remotest villages they are household characters. The reason is that unlike the *Iliad* and the *Odyssey*, these epics are not just adventure stories, they are the biographies of the gods who are worshipped to this day, and they are studded with philosophic and moral dissertations of so high a nature as to satisfy even the most modern and scientifically minded.

The *Ramayana* is the story of Prince Rama who went to Lanka (Ceylon) with the help of the monkey god Hanuman, to recover Sita his abducted wife from the clutches of the demon Rawana. It is also a story of filial brotherly love and wifely devotion and of virtue conquering evil.

The *Mahabharata* is the story of the war for the throne between the Pandava kings and their Kaurava cousins; all through the epic runs the concern of man for his place in the universe as well as the principle of causality.

It is in the *Bhagavad Gita* (the Song of the Lord), a part of the *Mahabharata*, that the Hindu doctrine is fully explained in a magnificent dialogue between man and his creator. Before the final battle of Kurukshetra (near what is now Delhi), Arjuna the Pandava hero has doubts. Is it right to fight and kill men who are his relations and his old friends, above all is war justifiable? The god Krishna in disguise argues with Arjuna, pointing out that the duty of a warrior is to fight in a righteous war. When he fails to convince him, throwing away his disguise, Krishna reveals himself to the hero and answers his questions on the nature of the universe, the way to God, and the meaning of duty.

God is the Known and the Knower, unmanifest and changeless, without beginning, eternal, immanent, all-pervading, the One without a Second. He is at once the sacrifice and the prayer, life and love, birth and death, the visible and the invisible. There are many ways to reach Him: through devotion, through works, through knowledge, and through mystic union. The man who wants to attain God must renounce all attachment, must accept both good and evil, heat and cold, praise and blame. He must be tied to no one and despise no one; doing his duty in this life according to his station.

God wins the argument and Arjuna goes to fight, without regret, without hatred, because he is a soldier and because his cause is just. But duty is not always as clear cut for Hindus as the *Bhagavad Gita* would imply. Thus, in the *Mahabharata*, the real hero is Bishma who is killed defending the Kaurava usurpers. Bishma is a philo-sopher-prince who has renounced all hatred and all ambition but who failed to persuade the Kauravas to hand back the kingdom to the rightful heirs, so he fights by their side out of a sense of loyalty and responsibility, knowing that he will be killed because it is not a just war.

Hinduism is directly derived from the epics, just as Christianity is directly derived from the Bible. Hinduism is much more than just a religion, it is a way of life; a framework for every individual action, for every decision, for every thought from the moment of birth to the moment of death. An orthodox Jew, like an orthodox Hindu, cannot exercise discrimination in what he accepts or rejects from this framework because, unlike some Christians, he does not have an organized church with authority to interpret ritual. However, since there is no religious authority, the unorthodox can reject what he likes. He can, for instance, eat pork or beef, without ceasing to be a Jew, or a Hindu.

For the orthodox Hindu the rules are all embracing; they lay down not only how often he must wash, but how he must wash, whom he can marry, what he can and cannot eat, with whom he can eat, when and how to shave, when to have sexual intercourse, how to relieve nature, how to earn a living. Such a strict ritual has the great advantage of providing the individual with a well defined blueprint for his whole life. This eliminates the great strains of decision making which individuals have to bear in the modern world. Hinduism weaves around the orthodox Hindu, even the Hindu Untouchable, the double cocoon of certainty and warmth of belonging, but this certainty and warmth are paid for in stagnation. The Hindu who rebels is thrown into a world where he must fight alone, surrounded by the hostility of those who have a vested interest in the *status quo*; a world so cold that only the bravest dare rebel.

However, Hinduism is much more than a code of conduct; it is also a philosophy which asserts the oneness of all creation and the immense importance for man to achieve mystical union with the Divine. In its abstract, philosophic form, Hinduism has no dogma. The definition of a Hindu is 'one who is born a Hindu'. A Hindu can be an atheist; or he can believe in all the thousands of gods and godlings which are but the many representations of the different aspects of the Divine; or he can believe in one God to the exclusion of all others and still be a Hindu. The orthodox Hindu view is that God is everywhere, in all things and all beings. There is, however, another equally orthodox Hindu view which holds that God, like life, is nothing but Maya, illusion. The reason for this elasticity of belief is that Hinduism has no church. The priests, as distinct from the sages, the scholars and the ascetics, are looked down upon because they are mere reciters of prayers, performers of ritual, feeders of the gods and beggars for alms. Hindu sages, scholars and saints are primarily concerned with their own enlightenment, with liberating themselves from the cycle of rebirths. They do not legislate or hold Conciles. This is why Hinduism remains flexible enough to run the whole gamut from the Upanishadic 'Lead me from the unreal to the real, lead me from darkness to Eternity' – with the emphasis on 'me', not 'them' as in Judeo-Christianity – to the most cruel animal sacrifices. From austerity to tantric worship; from contemplation to thuggee.

Yet, despite the infinite variety of Hindu interpretation and practice, some common beliefs put their unifying stamp on all Hindus. First, the belief in reincarnation is fundamental. Secondly, there is the belief in the eventual fusion of the individual into the Godhead, or into Nothingness, as the case may be, and the resultant deliverance from the cycle of rebirths. Thirdly, Hinduism is so elastic that it can absorb any kind of belief, from Christianity to Buddhism. The Buddha who preached against the Hinduism of his day ended up in the Hindu Pantheon as just another reincarnation of the god Vishnu. Finally, however indirectly, Hinduism postulates a belief in caste which is irretrievably linked to reincarnation and to the rigid causality which lays down that no cause is without effect, and that the thing which produces effect is action, not intention.

For most Hindus, Hinduism combines magic and witchcraft, belief in astrology, and the worship of domestic gods (like the Roman Lares and Penates). Day to day worship is mostly left to the women. Every Hindu home, even that of the modern educated, has its little temple, usually near the kitchen, where the family puts out its offerings and performs its worship. In addition the women often worship at the local temple, bringing their offerings of sweetmeats and flowers. They also go on distant pilgrimages, sometimes alone, sometimes with their whole family. Yet no matter how great a part idol worship plays in the life of the most orthodox and backward, all Hindus subscribe to the difficult doctrine of monism – the philosophic theory that all reality is one. This doctrine is evident even in the statues. Thus the Trimurthi represents Shiva, Vishnu and Brahma as *one* three-headed God; and there are representations of Shiva and Parvati as half-male, half-female statues. This is why the most devoted worshipper of a particular idol will take time off to explain that his particular idol is only one of the many representations of God in a particular mood and that God is both immanent and transcendent; but that for reasons of personal convenience, he worships the image of Hanuman, or Kali, or Devi, or Shiva.

Caste is the social manifestation of the underlying Hindu concepts of reincarnation, causality and duty. Basically there are four castes. A caste is best defined as a group of families whose members can intermarry and eat together without being polluted. The four original castes have split up over the ages into a jungle of subcastes, either because of occupation or because of heresy. The subcastes are firmly poised in the hierarchical social and religious ladder, if not on a national, at least on a regional basis. This elaborate system of precedence by which each group has a place above and below other groups, depends for its survival on acceptance. This acceptance is due to the belief in reincarnation by which one is born into a particular group as a result of the reward or punishment for one's actions in a previous life. Already by the time of Manu's Code, 2,000 years ago there were 50 castes. Today there are more than 2,000 Brahmin subcastes alone, while the Untouchables who, within their pariah fold, also follow caste practices, have more than 500 subcastes.

The subcastes only represent differences of degree, yet they remain as mutually exclusive as if they represented differences of kind. Brahmins who eat meat have nothing to do with those who eat fish, and vegetarian Brahmins regard both meat and fish eating Brahmins as almost Untouchable. Cultivators who use canal irrigation water keep at a safe distance from those who draw water from wells although both groups may grow identical crops. The potter who uses a small wheel to turn his pots has nothing to do with the potter who uses a large wheel in the same village.

It is caste which makes Indian society so unique. The whole group exists to ensure that each one of its members behaves properly; for on individual behaviour depends collective status. Improvements can only be achieved by the individual in after-life, through rein-carnation; or by the group as a whole, if its claim to higher status remains unchallenged. Since the groups function in water-tight compartments – not intermarrying or interdining – what a group does, so long as it does not impinge on another group, is a matter of concern only for the group itself. If cultivators wishing to upgrade their status decide to become vegetarians nobody objects; but if they wanted to learn the *Vedas* – in the old pre-British days a prerogative of the three top castes – they had their tongues cut out. The intran-sigeance of small groups is always extreme and the penalty for breaking the rules was expulsion. This in a society where marriage has to be within the group means that the culprit's entire family suffers. For instance, when Gandhi first went to study in England, the first Mod Bania to break the taboo of his subcaste on crossing the black waters, he and his family were excommunicated. As a result one of his nieces remained a spinster because her mother failed to find a son-in-law from the Mod Bania subcaste and was too orthodox to look outside the conventional range.

Because Hinduism is vague it has no rebels. Scientists can be good Hindus since there is nothing in Hinduism to prevent the reconcilia-tion of evolution with religion; while communists have no difficulty in reconciling dialectical materialism with reincarnation. But there have been rebels in the past against ritual, sacrifice and above all against caste.

The first rebel was Mahavira (540–467 B.C.) who founded Jainism. This sect does not recognize caste, deities or sacrifices and is pledged to the non-taking of life. All Jains are strict vegetarians; even the eating of roots is not allowed because they have to be pulled out of the ground. Jains make no distinction between the meanest insects and men. There have been riots to protest against locust extermination and some Jains run homes for bed-bugs, complete with paid human fodder. At one time the Jains ruled over large parts of India but now they are concentrated in western India.

The greatest Hindu reformer, however, was a young prince of the Warrior caste, who lived in northern India in the Kingdom of Kapilavastu. His father, who feared a prophecy according to which his only son would renounce the world, kept him prisoner in a little garden of Eden, surrounded by luxury and beauty. One day the young Prince drove his chariot through the city unannounced, and, for the first time in his life, saw an old man, a sick man, and a corpse. The shock was so great that he began to meditate on the meaning of life. Abandoning his beautiful wife who had just borne him a son he set out into the world to beg. After prolonged wanderings, studies and mortifications he arrived at Bodh Gaya in what is now Bihar. There, under a pipal tree, he was rewarded by illumination. From then on he became known as the Buddha (567–487 B.C.), the Enlightened One, and he began to preach a new religion.

Buddhism, which is over 2,500 years old, is one of the great religions of the world. From India it spread to the four corners of Asia: to Burma, Ceylon, Indonesia, Tibet, Indo-China, China and Japan. Like the Protestant Reformation in the West during the sixteenth century it is a reaction against the excesses of ritual. It preaches detachment, the abolition of caste and sacrifice, and the emptiness of human assertions about God. By the time the Buddha died in 487 B.C., he had made many converts and Buddhism flourished in much of India for the next 1,500 years, before it disappeared mysteriously. Perhaps the Buddha's ideas were taken over by the great Hindu philosopher Shankaracharya in the ninth century A.D. and were re-adapted to Hinduism so as to make Buddhism no longer necessary. Whatever the reason, the Buddha who had preached the absence of God became a Hindu god.

Little of what happened in India is known until the incursion of Alexander the Great who rode down the Indus Valley in 326 B.C. But Alexander had to turn back when his soldiers revolted. The Macedonians used horses and this gave them a great advantage against the elephants of the Hindus who were likely to turn on their own side. Alexander's successor was thrown out of the Punjab in 305 B.C. by Chandragupta Maurya who had usurped the throne of Magadha at the time of Alexander's raid.

IV   The Mauryans: 322 B.C.–185 B.C.

Our knowledge of Chandragupta's Empire is derived from the writings of the Greek Megasthenes who has left us an account of the splendour and order he saw.

It was Ashoka, Chandragupta's grandson (c. 273–232 B.C.), who brought the Mauryan Empire to its climax. He was both a great and good ruler and his rule extended over more than two-thirds of India but, in a number of places, this rule was only nominal. At first, following his grandfather's example he fought many wars. It is said that the conquest of Orissa resulted in 100,000 dead and 150,000 prisoners, while thousands died of pestilence and hunger. Stricken by remorse Ashoka became a Buddhist. He renounced war and governed his Empire according to the dictates of the Buddha, making Buddhism the official religion of the state. He sent missionaries to many lands, built Buddhist centres of learning, erected stone pillars ordering the proper treatment of slaves, human tolerance and prohibiting sacrifices. Shortly after Ashoka's death his Empire began to decline and a period of anarchy settled over northern India. There was nothing to prevent an invasion.

V   The Invasions: c. 185 B.C.–A.D. 320

Invasions came in successive waves from Central Asia. There were the Sakas, then the Kushans whose greatest king, Kanishka (c. A.D. 120–160), became a Buddhist and ruled northwestern India

21

and Afghanistan. Anarchy followed for a century and a half, until the rise of the Gupta dynasty.

VI *The Guptas and Harsha:* A.D. *320–647*

The Guptas were destined to be wiped out by the same Huns who invaded Europe under Attila. During the rule of the Guptas northern India enjoyed its Golden Age for nearly two centuries until anarchy once more settled over the whole country. For our knowledge of this period, the fog of history has been lifted by the Chinese traveller Fa Hien who studied Buddhism and stayed for a time at Pataliputra, the Gupta court. Fa Hien wrote of a peaceful, prosperous and well-administered empire. Gupta India was far in advance of any country in the known world. There was a great Buddhist university at Nalanda in Bihar, which attracted students from all over Asia. The university had eight colleges and three libraries.

India's contribution to the world tends to go unnoticed because much of it did not come directly to the West. Beside the Arabic numerals, the zero, and the decimal system, Indian metallurgy and chemistry was well ahead. Indian tempering of iron has not been equalled yet and nobody has been able to repeat the miracle of the rust-proof iron pillar which stands near Delhi. Everything Fa Hien wrote has been supported by the extraordinary quality of the sculpture and architecture of the period. Unfortunately little is known in the West because what has not been overgrown by jungle or destroyed by Muslims was labelled pornographic by the straight-laced Victorians.

It was during this Golden Age that the *Mahabharata* was written down and that, thanks to the perfection of the Sanskrit language, secular literature flourished. Beside Kalidasa whose *Shakuntala* is one of the great love plays of all time, there were many unknown writers who recorded the folk and fairy tales which have inspired Aesop, La Fontaine, Boccaccio and Shakespeare.

Of this glory all that remain, besides the literature, the statues, and the advancement of science, are ruins of temples and great irrigation works; for the Huns, as in Europe, brought the Dark Age in their wake.

2 Rajputs and Muslims

BY THE TIME MUSLIM TRAVELLERS and scholars visit the Rajputs, who were the rulers of all northern India from *c.* A.D. 800–1200, and leave their testimony the Indian scene has totally changed. Buddhism is no longer important. The great University at Nalanda has been destroyed; Hinduism is vigorous; and clan chieftains, claiming descent from the Sun, the Moon and the Fire, rule a series of kingdoms all over northern India behaving like the medieval knights, forever at war, forever in love, forever chivalrous, forever treacherous. Since actual descent from the Sun and the Moon is unlikely, they must either have been descended from Central Asian invaders who carved kingdoms for themselves and adopted Hindu, ism, or from tribal chiefs who, on conversion to Hinduism claimed a Warrior status not even Brahmins dared challenge.

According to these Muslim records, Sanskrit scholarship flourished under the Rajputs. Brahmins were powerful, women were educated and played an important part in public life although they were married very young. High caste women had to commit *suttee* (be burnt alive on their husband's funeral pyre) while lower, caste widows could not remarry and female infanticide was practised. People were very religious and went for regular pilgrimages to holy rivers and mountains. Laws were good, taxes mild – one, sixth of the produce of the land only – and for merchants there was an income tax. But the records are vague and patchy and we only know what happened to strike the imagination of the visitors.

It was however the Muslim Conquest which started in 1193 and lasted until the battle of Plassey in 1757 that has left its mark on

Indian history. This conquest was never complete, indeed it never extended to the extreme south at all; it was only continuous along the Gangetic Valley and in the Punjab. Over the rest of India, Muslim rule lay like clouds over a mountain range; patchy, uneven, at times a mere mist, at times a thick blanket, intermittent, unreliable. The Muslims did not inspire loyalty in their own followers who were always scrambling for position. Above all, since Islamic law does not recognize dynastic succession, court intrigues were always so rife that pretenders legitimate or otherwise had to look for the support of outsiders with the result that even at the height of their glory, the Muslims had to allow a certain amount of independence to those Rajputs who were on their side. Yet somehow the impression has been created, both in the world at large and in India itself, that the Muslim Empire in India was akin in its scope and legacy to the Roman Empire.

There are three reasons for this illusion. First, Hindu interest in history is almost non-existent with the result that there have been hardly any Hindu commentary or records for the period. Second, the historians of the Moghul Period were not merely Muslims but courtiers who, like courtiers the world over, took good care to sing the praise of their patrons and to overlook their weaknesses. This explains why there are so many epic descriptions of the way in which the Muslims took, time and again, the same Fort of Kalinjar, and why there is not one clue as to how they came to lose it so many times. (Presumably had there been Rajput historians equally epic descriptions would have been made of the many times they took the Fort of Kalinjar back.) Finally, the Muslims, perhaps because of the Quranic injunction against graven images, or because of the arrogance of victory, fairly systematically destroyed the temples and the palaces they conquered. Therefore because one sees so many mosques, tombs, and Muslim palaces one tends to exaggerate the importance of the Muslim period. The Hindus built no tombs and lived in the same palaces for generations, whereas the Muslims had to build separate tombs for each of their dead and also moved capital as often as their whims dictated. Moreover the Muslims had practically no impact on south India at all.

In southern India the history is even patchier. There were great dynasties. The Satyavahanas, the Pallavas, the Rashtrakutas, and the Chalukyas built great empires extending from Madras to Patna, but little is known about them. There seems to have been a kingdom in the eastern Deccan, a kingdom in the western Deccan, and two kingdoms in the Tamil country. These kingdoms were at war with each other from time to time, and sometimes a feudatory broke away to set up on his own. This state of affairs prevailed from the second century B.C. to the twelfth century A.D.

The kings in southern India were great irrigators; they built water tanks, they bunded lakes, and the Brahmins, who dominated in a way they never did in the north, owned large irrigated estates and amassed great riches. Art in the south flourished, as can be seen to this day from the great cave temples of Ellora and Ajanta, and the temples of Mahabalipuram and Halebid. In addition we know that the Tamil kings were great seafarers. In the Emperor Augustus' days they were trading with Rome to the equivalent of nearly one and a half million pounds (sterling) a year. They also sent ships to the whole of Southeast Asia, and with the ships went traders, monks and scholars who emigrated and gave to Southeast Asia its Hindu and Buddhist institutions.

Although there was no historical or political unity in India, there nevertheless existed, all over the subcontinent, and indeed beyond it in the rest of Southeast Asia, an underlying civilization based upon religion, culture and social organization. This culture was carried not by invaders but by Hindu priests, Buddhist monks, Indian traders, craftsmen, master builders and sculptors; thus the great temples of Angkor Wat in Cambodia, or Borobodur in Indonesia are Hindu both in conception and detail. And in India itself, whether north or south, Brahmins had everywhere the same recognized social place; they were scholars, priests or coveted cooks – since the food they handled could be eaten by everybody without fear of pollution. Indeed, it is upon the peculiar social structure of caste that Indian unity was built. Even if the castes remained water-tight, even if they varied from one place to another, their very exis-tence was something so special, so unique, that it forged a link between Indians; a link which distinguished them from all other people.

However, the Muslim Conquest made a profound impression on India because, for the first time in her long history of invasions and conquests, Hindu India did not assimilate the foreigner. Until the Muslims came to India, invaders and conquerors had a civilization and above all a religion less developed than that of the Hindus. Naturally, therefore, they were absorbed. But this was no longer true of the Muslims. The Muslims were militant and their religion was too dogmatic to be swallowed in the quicksands of Hinduism. So for the first time India failed to conquer its conqueror. Indeed because of the all embracing nature of Hinduism the only way the Muslims could protect themselves from assimilation was by an aggressive attitude which in its turn made the Hindus curl back into the protective shell of caste. As a result an uneasy coexistence between conquerors and conquered was struck; coexistence broken here and there by forcible conversion, marriage, or persecution.

The first Muslim onslaught came with Mahmud of Ghazni, who invaded India from Afghanistan 17 times, but failed to establish himself. It was left to Muhammad of Ghor to defeat the Rajputs in 1192 on the sacred field of Kurukshetra outside Delhi. Fourteen years later the Sultanate of Delhi was established, covering, very loosely, most of northern India. The Sultanate was too far flung and its lines of communication were too extended with the result that in due course it collapsed leaving nothing behind except stately tombs and extortionate taxes. From 1206 till 1526 the 27 Turkish kings who occupied the throne in Delhi were engaged in a series of dynastic blood feuds, and intermittent Hindu persecution. During this period Hindu culture declined, caste became more rigid, women were put into purdah to protect them against Muslim lust, and Urdu – the court language which is a cross between Persian and the local dialects – flourished. A minor school of painting also came into being.

While Muslim rule sprawled over northern India, at the mercy of the goodwill of its generals who had the habit of setting themselves up as suzerains the moment they could get away with it, in south⁄

west India a powerful Hindu kingdom made its appearance along the river Tungabhadra. This was the Vijayanagar Empire (1336–1585) whose existence protected southern India from any further Muslim depredation. The Muslim Sultans who surrounded Vijayanagar on the north finally defeated the Empire, not on behalf of their Delhi overlord, but on their own account; for by this time the Sultans of Delhi had ceased to have any real power.

Again and again, the moment power decayed in Delhi, India was invaded from the north. This is what happened when the Turk, Mohammed Babur, with 1,200 men on horseback defeated the last Sultan of Delhi at Panipat in 1526 and founded the Moghul Empire. This Empire lasted for two centuries, until the British took over.

Babur's grandson, the Emperor Akbar (1556–1605) was the first Muslim ruler who attempted to reconcile the Hindus to Muslim rule. He was also the first Indian ruler to work out an administrative system. Neither the reconciliation nor the administrative system survived him for long, although the latter did provide a pattern for the British to follow. From the time of Akbar the Moghuls married Hindu princesses in the attempt to make allies of the Rajputs who were prepared to put self-interest before the purity of their blood. The House of Udaipur which alone refused to give a daughter to the conquerors is to this day held in great respect above all other Rajput houses. Akbar divided northern India into twelve administrative provinces which were farmed-out to military governors responsible for the collection of land revenue. In a desperate effort to reconcile the Hindus, Akbar invented a composite religion of which he was the living God-Emperor. This religion died after him; it was equally unacceptable to orthodox Muslim and Hindu.

Akbar's political efforts were doomed to failure because like all Muslim rulers he could not establish a stable line of succession. His son Jehangir, a drunkard, owes his place in history to the fact that it was under his rule that the East India Company established its first foothold in India with a factory in Surat. The next Emperor, Shah Jahan, whose reign was marked by a continuing bloodbath, is remembered by the Taj Mahal, the admirable mausoleum built in memory of his wife, Mumtaz, who died giving birth to his fourteenth child. His son Aurangzeb (1618–1707), who killed most of his own family to make sure of the succession, began once more to persecute the Hindus and reintroduced the poll tax abolished by Akbar. Aurangzeb was the last of the great Muslim rulers. Although he never ruled India effectively, he contained the Marathas, and conquered Golconda, the last independent Muslim state. But disloyalty had become so widespread that when Aurangzeb died at the age of 89 he left an India ripe for anarchy. After his death the Marathas, who extended their base in western India as far as Delhi, were able to raid Calcutta and Bangalore whereas in the Punjab the Sikhs, a militant Hindu martial sect, were gaining ground. And all the time invasions from the north kept taking place; the Persians sacked Delhi in 1737 carrying away the Peacock Throne, the Afghans defeated the Marathas at Panipat in 1761. India had fallen prey to chaos – time was ripe for change.

This pillar which is today the symbol of the Indian Republic was built during the rule of Ashoka who extended the great Mauryan Empire over two-thirds of India in the third century B.C.

2 The underlying featur
of India's early history a
Buddhism and its pred
cessor Hinduism. This
the north gate of the Bu
dhist temple at Sanc
built in the first century B.

3 This group of bould
carved into Hindu shrin
at Mamallapuram date fro
the seventh century A.D.

4 Jainism, a sect which rebelled against the Hindu caste system, was founded in the sixth century B.C. and is still prevalent in western India. This massive statue of a Jain saint was made in the thirteenth century A.D.

5 During the thirteenth century northern India was divided into kingdoms ruled by clan chieftains. A relic of one such kingdom is this sculptured chariot wheel at the Konarak temple of the sun god.

6 This Buddhist cave painting of a Bodhisattva at the Ajanta cave in western India dates from the seventh century A.D.

7 An eighth-century relief of the Hindu gods Shiva and Parvati at the Ellora caves in western India.

8 The Moghul Empire was founded by the Turk Babur in 1526. His grandson (*right*) Akbar (1556–1605) attempted to reconcile Hindus to Muslim rule. From a nineteenth-century Moghul miniature.

9 During the rule of Jehangir (1569–1627), Akbar's son (*centre right*), the East India Company was established. From a nineteenth-century Moghul miniature.

10 (*far right*) When Aurangzeb (1618–1707), the last of the great Moghul rulers, died, India was ripe for anarchy. From an eighteenth-century Moghul miniature.

11 The Sikhs, a militant Hindu sect who increased their power in the seventeenth century, were founded in 1469 by Guru Nanak. A somewhat fanciful early twentieth-century painting of the birth of Guru Nanak.

12 A seventeenth-century Moghul miniature of a prince holding court.

13 At death the body of a Muslim is buried whereas that of a Hindu is burnt. A nineteenth-century engraving of a Muslim burial.

14 The remains of a Muslim tomb at Badami dating from the Moghul period.

15 This map illustrates the extent of the Moghul Empire in northern India during the seventeenth century.

16 A seventeenth-century English traveller brought back this impression of the Great Moghul, Aurangzeb.

17 The greatest monument to the Moghul period is the Taj Mahal mausoleum in Agra built by Shah Jahan (1592–1666) in the seventeenth century.

18 An eighteenth-century Moghul miniature of Shah Jahan.

3 The Company and the Empire

AFTER THE MOGHUL COLLAPSE India was waiting for a new master and there were five contenders: the French and the British who had a series of factories along the coast, the Nizam of Hydera/ bad, a rebel Muslim official who had set himself up on his own, the Sultan of Mysore, and the Maratha power. As the famous historian, Seeley put it, 'the British won in a fit of absence of mind'.

The conquest of India by Britain was not planned. The British were forced into India by her anarchy and the greed of Dutch traders.

Britain had no winter grazing; cattle had to be killed before winter and the meat preserved in salt. This meant that Britain was very dependent upon the spices from the East which were required to make salted meat palatable. So long as the spice trade remained in Portuguese hands, the British were quite happy to buy their spices from the Portuguese. But when the Dutch superseded the Portuguese in the East, they asked such exorbitant prices for spices that a small group of English traders formed themselves into the *Company of Merchants of London Trading into the East* under a Royal Charter dated 31 December 1600. The Company's capital was £70,000, and its 127 shareholders had secured from Queen Elizabeth I a 15/year spice monopoly.

The enterprise was purely commercial; nothing was further from the minds of the shareholders than conquest. But once the Company began operations in India its servants found that to protect their warehouses from the surrounding anarchy, they had to raise an armed force. This armed force was in due course drawn into taking sides in local Indian feuds; indeed by the time Britain and France were at war in Europe, the East India Company's soldiers were

37

fighting French troops and their Indian allies in India, to the despair of the Board of Directors of the Company in London.

Britons on the spot behaved like Indian rulers, extending their territory and assuming greater responsibility for law and order. And all this was at the expense of the Company's dividends which were swallowed up by the cost of running an empire.

At this point a chronology may be useful.

Chronology of the East India Company's Indian Take-over

The East India Company was chartered in 1600.

It established trading stations at Masulipatam in 1611, at Surat in 1612, and at Madras in 1641.

Its first piece of territory was acquired when it rented Bombay island from Charles II for £10 per year in 1668 (Bombay island was part of the dowry of his Portuguese wife Catherine of Braganza). It may be of interest to note that until 1857 the British crown possessed only Bombay island in India; the rest belonged to the Company.

Calcutta was founded in 1699 as a trading post.

During the Anglo-French wars of the mid-eighteenth century the Company defeated a series of French attempts to dominate south India between 1746 and 1760. As a result of these wars the Nizam of Hyderabad and the Nawab of the Carnatic became subordinate allies, and the Company acquired large stretches of the east coast.

The Nawab of Bengal captured Calcutta in 1756. The Company defeated the Nawab at Plassey in 1757 and put a puppet Nawab in his place. After the battle of Buxar in 1764 the Company was granted the Diwani of Bengal and the Viceroyalty of all eastern India by the Moghul Emperor. The Nawab of Oudh who ruled over what is now Uttar Pradesh, became a subordinate ally.

Wars with France during the Revolution and the Napoleonic period when Wellesley was Governor-General resulted in the further extension of the Company and the defeat of Tipu Sultan of Mysore.

Wellington defeated the Marathas in 1803 and from then on the Company ruled most of India although it required another war with Nepal 1814–16, another Maratha war in 1817–19, a war in

Sind in 1843, two wars in the Punjab (1845, 1848–9) and three wars in Burma (1824–6, 1852, 1886) before the process was complete.

The Mutiny broke out in 1857, the Crown took the East India Company over in 1858, and Queen Victoria was proclaimed Empress of India in 1878.

The British Take-over 1757–1858
India had been in contact with the West from the days of the Roman Empire but what had been a desultory trade in spices was transformed into a sustained trade when Vasco da Gama landed at Calicut in south India in 1498, to be followed in 1510 by Alfonso d'Albuquerque who established a Portuguese settlement in Goa. A century later Captain Hawkins landed at Surat and in a drinking contest won from Emperor Jehangir the right to establish trading posts in the towns of Surat, Ahmadabad and Masulipatam. Captain Hawkins, the East India Company's representative, was not interested in conquest. He wanted to be able to store pepper, cotton textiles, silks and calicoes in warehouses to await the seasonal ships which would take these commodities to Britain. Because of the collapse of law and order around the Company's warehouses, what had begun as trading posts had to be turned into forts; and soldiers had to be installed to protect them. Thus 'John Company', as the East India Company came to be known, first built Fort William in Bengal at a place which was later to become Calcutta, then Fort St George at what is now Madras. As the warehouses became fortified, Indian traders and artisans came to settle around them attracted by the promise of security from bandit raids and feudal wars. Thus, by the middle of the eighteenth century Madras had a population of a quarter of a million.

At first the East India Company made a great deal of money out of India. By 1740 Indian imports into Britain were worth one-tenth of the British government's revenue. This prosperity was due to the fact that Indians did not attack the traders and that the traders did not attack each other or intrigue against each other. Thus, throughout the War of the Spanish Succession, French and British traders coexisted peacefully; the French had their posts in Pondicherry and Chandernagore within a short distance of the British posts in Madras and Calcutta. But the War of the Austrian Succession (1740–8) changed all this. France and Britain sent fleets to India; the French took Madras in 1746 and the British attacked Pondi-cherry in 1748. At the peace Madras was given back to the British but the former spirit of coexistence was replaced by a new and militant spirit of cold war.

In order to strengthen his position, Dupleix, the French Governor-General of Pondicherry backed the Nizam of Hyderabad who had a feud with the Nawab of the Carnatic – his theoretical overlord from Moghul days. Hitherto the traders had kept themselves safely above local politics. Once the French had taken sides, the British, afraid of being pushed out by a victorious Nizam as a result of French assistance, chose, in order to protect their trading interests, to back the other side. Due to the help of an enterprising young captain, Robert Clive, the Nawab of the Carnatic defeated the Nizam. Four years later (1744) France and England were officially at war in Europe and therefore also in India. Pondicherry was captured by the soldiers of the East India Company, and returned to France at the peace.

But it was also during the Seven Years War (1756–63) that British influence spread over Bengal ending up with the formation of the Empire.

The events which led to British involvement in Bengal are very complicated. The British traders of Calcutta conspired against the Nawab of Bengal, Surajah Daulah, who reacted by taking Cal-cutta. Clive, who was in Madras, set off to avenge the traders. He fought the Nawab and defeated him at Plassey in 1757. The Nawab's army was 50,000 strong. Clive only had 2,000 men, properly drilled, whereas the Nawab's army was unreliable and the Nawab himself a coward. Mir Jaffar, the Nawab's Lieutenant, sided with Clive who rewarded him by making him Nawab of Bengal. Mir Jaffar was subsequently replaced by Mir Kasim who quarrelled with Clive and allied himself with the ruler of Ouhd and the Moghul Emperor; Clive had to fight Mir Kasim and his allies and defeated them at Buxar in 1764. In 1765 Clive obtained for the East India Company from the Moghul Emperor, the Diwani of Bengal, Bihar and Orissa, that is to say the right to collect taxes. British Rule in India had begun.

The Diwani proved so ruinous for the East India Company that within seven years of tax collection it had to ask the British government for a loan. But while the Board of Directors in London watched their dividends being swallowed up in administration, the Company's servants on the spot were getting rich at the expense of the people and famine broke out in Bengal.

Clive, who was told to put order into the Company's affairs, has left a telling description of those shameful days when Calcutta was:

> one of the most wicked Places in the Universe, Corruption, Licentiousness and a want of Principle seem to have possess'd the minds of all the Civil Servants, by frequent bad Examples they have grown Callous, Rapacious & Luxurious beyond Conception, & the Incapacity & Iniquity of some & the Youth of others. . . .

Clive's efforts were only partially successful and the men on the spot continued to amass fortunes. But whereas the Muslims in similar circumstances invariably revolted against central authority, set off on their own, carving kingdoms for themselves, the British employees of the Company did nothing of the sort. There were no attempts to assassinate Clive, no attempts to break away from the Board of Directors. On the contrary, they grudgingly accepted the limitations put by Clive on their profits and their graft so that, in due course, this very Company which had brought desolation to the countryside was to provide Britain with its Empire in India.

Warren Hastings, who was made Governor of Bengal in 1772, loved Indians and tried to put some order into the way the Company ruled Bengal. Above all he enlarged the Diwani by force of arms, defeating the Marathas and the Ruler of Mysore – a usurper helped by the French. But his activities did not meet with appreciation in London: Pitt the Younger by an Act of Parliament took over control of the East India Company and Hastings was impeached.

It was left to Cornwallis (1785–93), the first Governor-General of Bengal under Pitt's new Act, to bring about the changes Clive and Warren Hastings had initiated and to turn a merchant venture into a government. Cornwallis was a great aristocrat who had no connections with the East India Company. His first action was to insist that the Company's servants be properly paid and be answerable to the civil authority. In this way he laid the foundation of the Indian Civil Service. His next move, though inspired by the laudable desire to reproduce in India the squirarchy of Britain, was to prove a disaster for India. He introduced the Permanent Land Settlement by which Indian *zemindars* – the big Indian tax-farmers – became landlords. These newly created landlords let their agents squeeze the tenants, who had no redress. Thus a parasitic class of absentee landlords was created in Bengal and Madras where the Permanent Land Settlement was put into force. Fortunately in the rest of India the peasant remained, as before, a direct tenant of the government. Whenever the crops failed, the peasant got a remission of the land revenue, in a way he never did from the zemindar's agent whose sole interest was in how much he could squeeze out for himself, and for his master.

Cornwallis's policy had however one beneficial effect. By freeing the zemindars from living in the villages it created a class of men who in due course turned to Western education; men from whose midst were to arise the first Indians with enough vision to want to change their own society and thus pave the way for a modern India. At the same time, all over India, even in those areas where tenants were responsible to the government, land was becoming for the first time a marketable commodity. The result was that rents went up, indebtedness went up and many peasants were evicted while moneylenders became landlords. Under the old system land had belonged to the ruler and was not a marketable commodity.

The reforms begun by Cornwallis were carried on by Wellesley, the Duke of Wellington's brother, who was Governor-General from 1798 to 1805. Wellesley fought Tipu the Sultan of Mysore, who was killed in 1799 at Seringapatam. He installed in Mysore a friendly government, defeated the Marathas princes, and entered into a series of alliances with the ruling princes. The result of Wellesley's alliances was to make Britain the paramount power in India while the princes became vassals responsible only for local affairs.

Within six years of his arrival in India Wellesley had extended British rule over most of the subcontinent and had set up an Administrative College to train the Company's servants in the art of administration. Far from being rewarded, he was recalled in disgrace because the Company's dividends had fallen. His successor was ordered not to indulge in politics or territorial expansion, but to make money.

This was more easily said than done. Conditions on the spot were such that the Company could not remain passive. In order to protect its commercial interests it had to be drawn into action and expansion, whatever the official brief. The Centre of India was prey to Pindari lawlessness which threatened the entire subcontinent if it remained unchecked. The Pindaris, freebooter-auxiliary of the Marathas, roamed the land, killing and looting everything they found. An English traveller described them thus:

> The Pindaris were neither encumbered by tents or baggage. Each horseman carried a few cakes of bread for his horse. The party which usually consisted of two or three thousand good horses with a proportion of mounted followers, advanced at the rapid rate of forty or fifty miles a day, neither turning to right or left until they arrived at their destination. They then divided, and made a sweep of all the property and cattle they could find; committing at the same time the most horrid atrocities, and destroying what they could not carry away . . . before a force could be brought against them they were on their return.

Their number was so great that it took 100,000 Company soldiers to defeat them. The Maratha princes, whose auxiliary the Pindaris were, naturally came to the rescue of their friends. The Company therefore had to defeat them in the 1818 war, further extending its territory and responsibilities. By this time the Company held sway over most of India, either directly or through vassal princes. Only Kashmir, Assam, the Punjab and Sind were still left to conquer.

Until Lord William Cavendish-Bentinck came as Governor-General in 1828, the British in India had not interfered with Indian customs. They had concentrated on trade, conquest and raising the standard of behaviour of their own representatives. Hindu and Muslim traditions had been left untouched. But by the time Lord Bentinck came to India there were already a few Indians like Ram Mohan Roy (see page 51) sufficiently Westernized and enlightened to want to introduce social reform and to back the new Governor-General in his drive to rid India of her more barbaric customs. Under Lord Bentinck, suttee and child infanticide were made illegal. Thuggee and child sacrifice were abolished. Suttee was practised only by the higher castes, girl infanticide was largely a Rajput practice to avoid the financial burden of providing daughters with an adequate dowry. Child sacrifice was an aboriginal practice. Thugs belonged to a brotherhood which strangled people in order to please Kali, the goddess of destruction. These negative reforms however did not arouse as much hostility as did Bentinck's positive reforms; the most important of these was the principle of equality before the law.

Equality before the law was revolutionary in a country where society was divided by caste, where punishments were decided not by the gravity of the offence but by the caste of the offender. Thus a Brahmin could never be put to death no matter what his crime; whereas an Untouchable would be killed for an offence for which a Brahmin might be fined or exiled. Equality before the law challenged the whole social structure of India. But Lord Bentinck was determined to build 'British greatness upon Indian happiness', and if happiness was to be for all, Indian society had to be adapted to the British model. Lord Bentinck was not alone in holding these views as can be seen from Macaulay's famous Minute on Education. Macaulay told Parliament on 10 July 1835 that he wanted to create a class of:

Indians in blood and colour, but English in taste, opinions, morals, and intellect (because) no nation can be perfectly well governed till it is competent to govern itself. It may be that the public mind of India may expand under our system till it has

44

outgrown that system . . . that by good government we educate our subjects into a capacity for better government, so that they may demand European institutions. Whether such a day will ever come I do not know. Whenever it comes, it will be the proudest day in English history. There are triumphs which are followed by no reverses. There is an empire exempt from all natural causes of decay, the imperishable empire of our arts and our morals, our literature and our laws.

The policy Macaulay proposed was as revolutionary as his vision; Indians were to be given the benefit of an English education from secondary school onwards, government business was to be carried out in English, and colleges were to be opened. The old society was indeed under threat. How severe this threat was is shown by the fact that this new policy made modern India possible because it created the middle class from which were to rise the fighters for freedom, and which was to become sufficiently broadbased for India to make a success of the democratic experiment after Independence. Macaulay was consistent. In 1833 he had already told Parliament:

It would be, on the most selfish view of the case, far better for us that the people of India were well-governed and independent of us than ill-governed and subject to us; that they were ruled by their own kings, but wearing our broadcloth, and working with our cutlery, than that they were performing their salaams to English collectors and English magistrates, but were too ignorant to value, or too poor to buy, English manufactures. To trade with civilized men is infinitely more profitable than to govern savages. That would indeed be a doting wisdom, which, in order that India might remain a dependency, would make it a useless and costly dependency; which would keep a hundred millions of men from being our customers in order that they might continue to be our slaves.

And Macaulay was neither alone nor the first Briton to hold this view. Ten years earlier, Elphinstone, the founder of the Indian education system, had written to a friend in England:

It is I think our very first duty, and it will be better for us to lose the country by the effects of our liberality than to keep it . . . not that I think the immediate danger of our losing the country increased by education, on the contrary, the immediate danger is much diminished. But there can be no doubt that when the natives get more extended notions they will expect first a share of their own government and then the whole.

Sir Charles Trevelyan, a servant of the Company, expanded this theory in his pamphlet: *Education in India*:

The existing connexion between two such distant countries as England and India, cannot, in the nature of things, be permanent: no effort of policy can prevent the natives from ultimately regain-ing their independence. But there are two ways of arriving at this point. One of these is through the medium of revolution; the other, through that of reform. In the one, the forward movement is sudden and violent; in the other, it is gradual and peaceable. One must end in the complete alienation of mind and separation of interests between ourselves and the natives; the other in a permanent alliance, founded on mutual benefit and good-will. The only means at our disposal for preventing the one and securing the other class of results is, to set the natives on a process of European improvement, to which they are already sufficiently inclined. They will then cease to desire and aim at independence on the old Indian footing. . . . The political education of a nation is a work of time; and while it is in progress, we shall be as safe as it will be possible for us to be. The natives will not rise against us; we shall stoop to raise them; there will be no reaction, because there will be no pressure; the national activity will be fully and harmlessly employed in acquiring and diffusing European know-ledge, and in naturalizing European institutions. The educated classes, knowing that the elevation of their country on these principles can only be worked out under our protection, will naturally cling to us. . . . The change will thus be peaceable and gradually effected; there will be no struggle, no mutual exaspera-tion; the natives will have independence, after first learning how to make good use of it; and we shall exchange profitable subjects for still more profitable allies. . . . Trained by us to happiness and independence, and endowed with our learning and political institutions, India will remain the proudest monument of British benevolence; and we shall long continue to reap, in the affectionate attachment of the people, and in a great commercial intercourse with their splendid country, the fruit of that liberal and enlightened policy which suggested to us this line of conduct.

Another great administrator was the Marquis of Dalhousie (Governor-General 1848–56) to whom India owes the development of her communications and agriculture. He built the Grand Trunk Road which goes from Calcutta to Peshawar via Delhi, he developed the ports, he built giant irrigation works and the first railways. At last India was being developed instead of being exploited by her British overlord.

Meanwhile the policy of non-expansion laid down in London was reversed and the Governor-General was encouraged to round off the area under his control; Sind was annexed in 1843, the Punjab was taken from the Sikhs in two wars (1846, 1849), and a British expedition was sent to Afghanistan where it failed.

It is indeed unfortunate for Indo-British relations that by the time the British had at last unified India and begun to develop it, living up to the doctrine of trusteeship on which mid-nineteenth-century imperialism was based, relations between Britons and upper-class Indians began to deteriorate.

So long as the British were merely traders there was little difference between them and the Indians with whom they had to deal; the standards of behaviour of eighteenth-century Britain were not so different from those of eighteenth-century India. Moreover, as there was not a great gap between the civilizations of Europe and India, there was little room for superiority complexes. The traders did not display colour prejudice and there was a great deal in common between their attitude to tiger-shoots and women and that of the ruling Indian princes. But as the East India Company began to change, as merchant adventurers were replaced by a managerial *élite*, so the gap widened, especially when steam navigation made it possible for the Company's servants to bring their wives with them from Britain. Respectable Indian women did not come out into mixed society so that the social gap was further widened by the attitude of British women who frowned upon dancing girls and created through their clubs little British oases in which there was no room for Indians of any sort. Contact between Indians and Britons became confined to the requirements of administration and domes- ticity. Later on the Mutiny was to isolate the British even more because it wove a cocoon of fear between rulers and ruled. By the time Indians were ready to mix with the British the pattern was set; they were excluded from clubs and railway carriages and naturally resented it bitterly. The very men and women who, in different circumstances would have been the supporters of the British, were the very people who became hostile.

The Mutiny (1857) was the climax of a process of alienation and suspicion which had been going on ever since William Bentinck and Macaulay's far-sighted policies undermined India's traditional society.

The spark which set off the Mutiny was in itself trivial: a rumour spread amongst Indian troops that the cartridges of their new Enfield rifles were greased with animal fat. The cartridges had to be bitten off, and animal fat, a mixture of pig and beef fat, is taboo for Muslims and Hindus since Muslims regard the pig as impure while Hindus regard the cow as sacred. However, the cartridges were only a pretext. Discontent had been widespread for a long time. There had been dissatisfaction in the Bengal Army – recruited very largely amongst Brahmins and Warriors – because British officers did not make sufficient allowances for the taboos of caste, particularly for the taboo on crossing the black waters; there had already been a small mutiny when a unit refused to fight in Rangoon during the Burmese War of 1824. Muslims too were disgruntled at being made to fight fellow Muslims in the Afghan war of 1839. To make discontent more discontented, there had been serious arrears in the payment of troops, and a feeling amongst Indian soldiers that British officers wanted to convert them to Christianity. Those who saw in the extension of British rule a threat to their age-old privileges actively fanned the soldiers' grievances, and raised the cry of religion in danger. Indeed, orthodoxy was being threatened by the advent of the railways which was making it impossible for Brahmin and Untouchable to keep their ritual distance in overcrowded carriages. The new law making it possible for widows to remarry threatened to divide inheritance, while the law by which Christian converts could claim a share of the family property was seen by all as a missionary plot.

Despite widespread resentment, the Mutiny lasted only one year, and did not spread beyond a third of the Indian Army and a few centres in northern India.

Until 1857 when the Mutiny broke out, the Indian Army had been divided into three units: the Bengal Army, largely drawn from the Province of Oudh in the Gangetic Valley, and the Bombay and Madras Armies – who remained loyal. The three armies put together consisted of 40,000 Britons and 200,000 Indians. In 1856 the British annexed Oudh and introduced land reforms which profoundly upset the landlords who could no longer exploit their tenants; there was a revolt in Oudh which naturally found its echo in the Bengal Army, so many of whose soldiers were precisely the same people who had lost their feudal privileges. The centres of the Mutiny – which was never much more than an Oudh revolution – were Meerut, Lucknow, Cawnpore and Delhi. The mutinous army was assisted by the Moghul princes, the Nana Sahib, the Rani of Jhansi and General Tantia Topi, who all got drawn in as the fighting continued but were not in any way conspiring confederates. All the other princes remained loyal and so did the rest of the Indian Army. The new Western-educated class of Bengal was the first to condemn the mutineers.

The Mutiny, which Indians call their First War of Independence, was to make a profound impact on India and on Indo-British relations. Although at no time did it look as if the mutineers would win, the shock in Britain was profound. Tales of sepoys killing their own officers, of British children and women murdered, had an almost Red-Indian Scalp-War horror about them – horror magnified by the fact that Britain was at last cosy, comfortable and Victorian. In the excitement caused by stories of heroism and treachery nobody realized that the Mutiny had not spread to most of India; indeed outside the Gangetic Valley nobody had shot anybody, and in the big centres of Calcutta and Bombay life had gone on as before.

In India itself the Mutiny increased the social gap between Britons and Indians; in the north splendid isolation was replaced by fear. The Bengal Army was disbanded, Indians were debarred from serving in the artillery; preferential recruitment was given to Sikhs and to Gurkhas from Nepal because they had remained loyal.

However, the key change brought about by the Mutiny was the winding up of the East India Company. In 1858 the British Parliament took over the Government of India and twenty years later, when ten-years-old Gandhi was already at school, Disraeli proclaimed Victoria Empress of India. The Empire was to be short-lived, but its impact on British minds was to be profound. It is the irony of history that in the British defeat of the Mutiny lay the foundation for Indian independence because the victor was not Britain but social change. But for the Mutiny the leadership of India would have remained with the old fashioned, the princes, the land-lords and the Sanskrit scholars who had a vested interest in the *status quo*. The Mutiny proved to everybody that the old order was doomed; it cleared the field for the Westernized middle class which was just beginning to take advantage of British education and was learning, from British books, to agree with Gladstone that good government is no substitute for self-government. It is no accident that the men who were to take India into freedom came from families who had not participated in the Mutiny. It is indeed an interesting fact that nobody who mattered politically in India by 1947, could boast a grandfather who had mattered at all. The new middle class was now looking to the British to free them from the shackles of orthodoxy and the abuse of caste, but they were to be bitterly disappointed; one of the reasons which made them go into politics against the British was that they decided to do for India what the British were by now too scared to do.

The British had learnt their lesson; they could not forget that the

Mutiny had been a reaction against social reform. From now on they were extremely careful not to interfere with society. For the ninety years the British government was to rule India, nothing was done to upset Hindu or Muslim custom and the princes were treated as faithful allies under paramountcy – a series of treaties by which they were given a free hand so long as they backed British rule. Because of paramountcy, a third of the subcontinent remained feudal and autocratic long after parliamentary democracy had been introduced to British India.

However, although the British did not live up to the expectations of those Indians who looked to the Magna Carta and John Stuart Mill for their model, their presence in India made it possible for the Indians themselves to introduce social reforms. Such reforms in pre-British days would have been unthinkable because no sooner had a potential reformer spoken than he would have been jailed or killed.

The first Indian social reformer, the most influential before Gandhi, was Ram Mohan Roy (1774–1833), whose real impact was felt after his death when enough Indians were sufficiently Westernized to want to change their own society. Ram Mohan Roy came from a family of Bengali landlords. He spoke ten languages and studied philosophy, science and comparative religion. For a while he worked for the East India Company, then he became a mystic, and finally he became a social reformer. Prior to Macaulay's policy on education he founded a college in Calcutta to teach Western techniques to Hindus. He also edited the first Indian newspaper. He attacked the caste system and founded the Brahmo Samaj, a Hindu casteless sect. It was at Ram Mohan Roy's instigation that suttee was abolished. He fought against idol worship and preached civil liberties. Finding the British in India too timid, he went to Britain to plead for more vigorous social reforms for his country. The Brahmo Samaj did not make many converts. It remained a Bengali upper-caste brotherhood – almost a caste dedicated to the non-recognition of caste – but its influence on Hindu thought was considerable; for the first time Hindu thought had been translated into Western actions. A link was therefore forged between East and

West, making it possible for Indians, who wanted to learn from the West, to retain their self-respect.

Ram Mohan Roy was followed by other social reformers. In the Punjab a militant Hindu sect called the Arya Samaj arose, while in Bengal the Rama Krishna Mission, based on a mixture of Hinduism and Protestantism, grew up. However, the most influential movement was to become the Theosophical Society under the leadership of Mrs Annie Besant, an Irish Home Ruler. The Theosophical Society had a small membership but its influence stemmed from the fact that it provided a philosophic meeting ground for Europeans and Indians; this was very important in rousing Indian nationalism at the turn of the century. Mrs Besant was to become the first woman to be President of the Indian National Congress.

Under the impact of Western values the Hindu conscience had been stirred by Ram Mohan Roy into feeling a need for reform. The Muslim conscience was awakened by Sir Sayyid Ahmed Khan.

The Muslims, unable to forget that they had ruled over the Hindus, felt frustrated at the way in which the Hindus were taking advantage of the new opportunities offered by British rule. Moreover, the Muslims resented the British who had displaced them and sulked in their feudal estates, taking no part in the economic revolution which was slowly gripping India. Sir Sayyid Ahmed Khan, who felt that Muslim salvation could only come through modern education, founded the Muslim University of Aligarh in 1875; and his efforts were to culminate in 1947 in the creation of Pakistan, a state for the Muslims of India. Sir Sayyid Ahmed Khan was a remarkably far sighted man, he saw – long before anybody else in India – that the purpose of British rule was to lay the foundations for a self-governing, democratic India. He therefore warned his co-religionists that they must have a state of their own if they were to be equal because democracy in India would inevitably mean rule by the Hindu majority. It was left to fiery Mohamed Ali Jinnah to bring into bloom the seed of Pakistan planted by the Muslim educationalist.

Before going into the details of British rule in India it may be useful to look at the chronology of the various steps which were, cumulatively, to lead to the transfer of power in 1947.

Chronology of events prior to 1947

1861 Legislative Councils were created at the Centre and in the Provinces (some Indian representatives were included in both)

1885 Indian National Congress founded and received a Viceregal blessing

1892 Some of the seats in the Legislative Councils were made elective

1909 The Morley-Minto Reforms increased Indian representation and the elective element; introduced Indians to the Executive Councils at the Centre and in the Provinces; and provided separate electorates for Muslims

1917 The British government formally declared that self-government was the objective for India

1919 The Government of India Act widened the electorates and gave all legislatures an elected majority with Indian ministers in charge of the nation-building subjects in the Provinces

1935 The Act of 1935 handed over the Provincial governments to Indian politicians with only reserved powers for the Governor. It also provided for a Federal Centre open both to the Provinces and the Indian states, with the Viceroy in charge of Defence, Foreign Affairs and Finance.

1942 Cripps offer rejected

1946 A Cabinet Mission from Britain visited India

1947 Power transferred to India by the British on 15 August

Chronology of the rise of nationalism

1885 Indian National Congress founded

1897 First terrorist outbreak

1905 Bengal partitioned

1906   Muslim League founded
1908   Tilak convicted of sedition
1911   Bengal reunited
1919   Trouble started in the Punjab
1920-2, 1931-2, 1934   Civil Disobedience Movements
1939   Congress Ministries resigned over the war
1940   Muslim League committed itself to Pakistan
1942   'Quit India' movement launched by Congress

From 1858 to 1947 the subcontinent was governed by a Viceroy under a Secretary of State for India – a Cabinet Minister – responsible to Parliament. A small cadre of dedicated and properly trained officials were recruited to run India. There never were more than 4,000 of them including the police, the railways, the forestry department and the engineers. In addition there were British officers in the Indian Army and a British Army which was originally composed of some 70,000 men, but was reduced to 40,000 by the 1930s.

For administrative purposes India was divided into 250 districts; the primary job of the administration in the district was to maintain law and order and to collect revenue. At the top of the administrative machinery was the Indian Civil Service (ICS for short). There were never more than 1,200 in the ICS and by the time India became independent nearly half of these were Indian. It is to the ICS that India owes her stability, the continuity of her institutions and the fact that of all the newly independent countries she is the most able to develop on modern lines. Members of the ICS were recruited from the cream of Britain's intellectual *élite*; the best brains at Oxford and Cambridge. So great was the reputation of the ICS that those who topped the list of the joint Home and Indian Civil Service list often chose India. Their high standard of integrity and their devotion to the country they served have been matched nowhere, not even in Whitehall. Perhaps this was because they were in such close contact with the people they ruled and loved so much – the peasants – who looked to them for justice and protection with such a compelling faith that it inevitably brought the best out of them. But dedication is not everything and the British in India

54

are open to the criticism that, although what they did, they did well, they did not do enough. These were the days of economic *laissez-faire* and men who went out to India fresh from universities and public schools were not likely to develop trade or industry; enthusiasm for the Criminal Procedure Code or the Classification of Castes and Tribes is seldom to be found coupled with an interest in pioneering industrial development. Nevertheless, the first four decades of British rule in India were marked by a great development of the best colonial kind. By 1900 there were 25,000 miles of railways and 14 million acres of land under irrigation – the biggest irrigation development in the world; in the universities there were 23,000 students, famines had practically been stopped, jute manufacturing and cotton textile industries were providing employment for the workers who were beginning to flock into the cities. Meanwhile Indianization of the lower rungs of the administration had been completed and a few Indians had gone into the ICS. Most of them, however, preferred to go in for the law, which seemed peculiarly well-suited to the Indian turn of mind. It can indeed be argued that had more Indians gone into the ICS, India would have been deprived of the leadership which was to challenge British rule at the end of the First World War.

As Indians became more and more familiar with British ways they were encouraged to voice their grievances. The Indian National Congress was founded by a retired ICS officer, A. O. Hume. The purpose was to provide a focus for political activities within the framework of British rule. However, for a long time the Indian National Congress remained primarily an expression of the views of the liberal middle class. It was not until Gandhi arrived on the scene that the Congress became a mass movement with which the British had to come to terms.

The culmination of British rule was the Viceroyalty of Lord Curzon from 1899 to 1905. Curzon was an empire builder; he consolidated the Afghan frontier, strengthened the administration, introduced a department of agriculture, protected the Punjabi peasant from the moneylender, added 6,000 miles to the railways and 6½ million acres to the land under irrigation, reorganized the army, and created the Archaeological Department to which Indian monuments owe their preservation and indeed sometimes their discovery. Unfortunately for Indo-British relations however, Curzon was arrogant and despised Hindus. He dismissed the Indian National Congress which he saw 'tottering to its fall' and hoped to 'assist it to a peaceful demise'. This did not seem such a vain hope at the time, for the Congress was then far from vigorous. However, it was the Viceroy himself who was to give life to the Congress.

The Province of Bengal, with 78,000,000 people, nearly half the population of British India, had become unwieldy; on the advice of his civil servants, Curzon decided for the sake of administrative efficiency to partition Bengal into two provinces, East Bengal and West Bengal. Bengali sentiment was outraged and for the first time since the British had arrived in India there was an outburst of genuinely modern nationalism – in sharp contrast to the Mutiny – which gave Congress its first chance to become known on an all-India scale. In Bengal itself there was an outburst of terrorism. Six years later in 1911 Bengal was reunited by Curzon's successor who solved the administrative problem by separating off the non-Bengali speaking areas of Bihar, Assam and Orissa, while leaving Bengal proper as one unit. But by then it was too late; patriotism had come to stay.

Curzon, the cause of the trouble, had quarrelled with his Commander-in-Chief; as a result he resigned and left India at the very time when events were occurring in East Asia which shook the world and undermined the Asian belief in Western supremacy. In the Russo-Japanese war the Japanese won; the first time an Asian power had defeated a European one. The myth of white superiority, the myth upon which British rule in India largely rested, was exploded.

The Bengali terrorists were not effective. The memory of Pindari depredations was still too fresh for most Indians to have much sympathy for men who took the law into their own hands and killed innocent victims in the name of the motherland. The Indian National Congress Party itself almost split over the rights and wrongs of the use of violence. At the head of the moderates who condemned it unequivocally was Gokhale, a Brahmin from Poona and a great social reformer who founded the Servants of India Society and became Mahatma Gandhi's political mentor. At the head of the extremists was Tilak, another Brahmin from Poona, a great educationalist and journalist who supported Hindu orthodoxy and coined the slogan 'self-government is my birthright'. Gokhale, who was in harmony with traditional Hindu tolerance, had much more following than Tilak, especially since most of India's newly created middle class was still grateful to British rule not only for law, order and education, but also for having made the existence of such a class possible. However, in 1909 the British government, following the policy of intimidation initiated by Lord Curzon, made Tilak a national hero overnight by sentencing him to six years imprison-ment for inciting people to violence. From then on, in India, as indeed in the rest of the British Empire, the pattern was set: politi-cians, in order to become national heroes, had to be put in the imperialist's jail. After Tilak's release, he was unanimously elected President of the Congress Party which he remained until his death when Gandhi took his place.

The argument between Gandhi and the British which was to fill over a quarter of a century with cajoling, praising, preaching, criticizing, heckling, haggling, jailing and fasting was not about outcome but about pace. Gandhi thought that India was already fit for self-government; the British government, imbued with its sense of trusteeship, thought that self-government should be intro-duced more slowly; but even at the height of the controversy dis-agreement was never over more than a generation at the outside.

Ever since Macaulay's famous Minute on Education the British government had been preparing India for self-government and ultimately for independence. It is sometimes forgotten that independence for British colonies had, in the light of Britain's experience with the United States and later with Canada, come to be regarded as the natural outcome of Imperialism.

Already in 1858 Queen Victoria's Proclamation had set out the right of every subject of the Queen, regardless of colour, caste or creed, to the appointment of any office under the Crown. From 1861 onwards Indians had been appointed to the Legislative Councils. By the 1880s Lord Ripon the Viceroy, in the teeth of local British opposition, had insisted that Indian magistrates were competent to try Europeans and had introduced partially elected local authorities – it is befitting that his statue in Calcutta was entirely paid for by Indians. From 1892 onwards the Viceroy's Legislative Council was encouraged to ask questions and discuss the budget. In 1909 an important advance was made when the Morley-Minto Reforms greatly increased the numbers of Indians elected to the Viceroy's Legislative Council and provided for one Indian Member in the Viceroy's Council, the equivalent of the British Cabinet. These reforms which laid the foundation of the Indian Parliament, also provided for partly Indianized Executive Councils (Cabinets) in the Provinces, and at the same time increased the degree of the local autonomy of the provincial governments. Moreover, the reforms created separate electorates for Muslims.

This provision was the result of the British feeling that the Muslim minority had the right to its fair share of the power which was now being delegated to Indians, and that, unless they were given separate electorates, they would be too backward as well as too dispersed to stand up to the majority. However, as could have been anticipated, the creation of separate electorates resulted in the exaggeration of Hindu-Muslim differences; the Muslim candidates for the separate seats did not have to bother about Hindu voters and were thus free to play on the religious emotions of a people who could not forget that the Muslims had once ruled India, and looked upon Hindus as 'idol worshippers'. From separate electorates to the creation of Pakistan, therefore, was merely a question of time and the slow hardening of attitudes. Nothing, however, was further from British intention than to divide India.

When Britain entered the war of 1914, India found herself automatically at war too. A large contingent of Indian troops was recruited on a voluntary basis and, at last, India's industrialization began to speed up. Hitherto, except for tea plantations, jute mills and some cotton mills the Indian economy had continued on more or less traditional lines. Now that communications with Britain were threatened, there was a better opportunity than there had ever been before to start textile mills, ordnance factories and railway workshops. There were also more Indian businessmen than there had been hitherto who were capable of taking advantage of this opportunity; there were plenty of those peasants not needed on the land to provide the labour; and plenty of war profits to provide the capital. In the excitement of the joint venture of war there was a short-lived explosion of mutual goodwill. In 1917 the Secretary of State for India, Edwin Montagu, told the British Parliament:

The policy of His Majesty's Government, with which the Government of India are in complete accord, is that of the increasing association of Indians in every branch of the adminis-tration and the gradual development of self-governing institutions with a view to the progressive realization of responsible govern-ment as an integral part of the British Empire. . . . I would add that progress in this policy can only be achieved by successive stages. The British Government and the Government of India, on whom the responsibility lies for the welfare and advancement of the Indian peoples, must be judges of the time and measure of each advance, and they must be guided by the co-operation received from those upon whom new opportunities of service will thus be conferred and by the extent to which it is found that con-fidence can be reposed in their sense of responsibility.

Montagu, who was due to visit India soon afterwards, ended by saying that substantial steps to give India more self-government would be taken shortly.

The Act of 1919 embodied some major advances towards self-government. The Viceroy's Council was to be enlarged to six Members besides the Commander-in-Chief, and three of the Members were to be Indian. The Legislative Council was to be replaced by a bi-cameral legislature consisting of a Legislative Assembly of 146 members, 106 of whom were to be elected, and of a Council of State partly elected on a restricted franchise. In the Provinces, for the first time, Indians were to become Ministers and were to be entrusted with the nation-building subjects; at the same time the officials, under the Governor, maintained the Reserved Subjects of Finance, Police, and Home. Franchise was on a property basis, irrespective of sex. During the next quarter of a century these Legislative Assemblies were to provide the training ground for the politicians who were to make such a success of Indian democracy.

Had the Act taken effect in 1917, in the fresh flush of Indo-British goodwill, the history of India might have been different; but the year 1919 was no longer auspicious. Far from welcoming the Act, the Indian politicians turned unco-operative.

The First World War was drawing to its close, and people every-where had been shaken from their feeling that the world was changeless. The Russian Revolution was putting the established order under threat; Lenin's pamphlet on 'Imperialism' was giving credence to the new theory of 'Capitalist Imperialist exploitation'; and in India itself, to bring tension to a head, the government was engaged in an unsuccessful war with Afghanistan. In the process of this war India was tightening on security because of a terrorist wave in the Punjab, on its lines of communications to Afghanistan.

By an irony of history the government of India's announcement of the 1919 Act coincided with the publication of the Rowlatt Bills; and the Bills overshadowed the Act. The Bills gave the government special powers to enable it to suppress subversion. In view of the repercussion these special powers were to have on Indian politics it is interesting to note that they were never used by the government.

Indian nationalists protested vehemently against the Rowlatt Bills; and when the Bills became Acts, the protest took the form of demonstrations which produced a chain reaction of shootings in Delhi, followed by the killing of four Britons in Amritsar, and culminating in the Jallianwallah Bagh shooting in which nearly 400 Indians were killed and some 1,200 injured, because they did not disperse. The meeting had been banned; the order to disperse was therefore perfectly proper but the British officer in command, General Dyer, did not know, when he gave his troops the order to shoot, that the guns were pointing at the only exit of the meeting ground.

The Jallianwallah Bagh shooting was effective in restoring law and order to the Punjab where the British had no trouble for the next 25 years. In the rest of India the effect was disastrous; it alienated many intellectuals, amongst whom was Nehru, and pushed Gandhi into non-co-operation. From then on relations between Britons and Indians were never the same, and it had clearly become merely a matter of time before Britain would have to face the dilemma anticipated by Professor Seeley in 1883 in his book *The Expansion of England* when he wrote that:

> We could subdue the Mutiny of 1857, formidable as it was, because it spread through only a part of the army, because the people did not actively sympathize with it, and because it was possible to find native Indian races who would fight on our side. But the moment a mutiny is but threatened, which shall be no mere mutiny, but the expression of a universal feeling of nationality, at that moment all hope is at an end, as all desire ought to be at an end, of preserving our Empire. For we are not really conquerors of India, and we cannot rule her as conquerors; if we undertook to do so, it is not necessary to enquire whether we could succeed, for we should assuredly be ruined financially by the mere attempt.

By the end of the Second World War there were no Indian races who were ready to fight for Britain to stay. Under Gandhi's brilliant strategy, nationalism had become too widespread. There were still many Indians who wanted the British to stay, but since their support was passive, it did not count and the British themselves, weakened by the war and harassed by Gandhi, had lost the will to stay.

Mohandas Karamchand Gandhi was born in 1869 in Porbandar, a small princely state on the coast of Kathiawar in western India. He was the youngest son of the Prime Minister, who was a merchant by caste. The Gandhis were very orthodox. Gandhi's mother, who had a profound influence on her son, was both a devout Hindu and so loath to the use of violence that, like the Jains whose influence is strong in that part of India, she observed the strictest vegetarianism. Gandhi was married at 13. Soon after his marriage he lost his father. Had it not been for his mother's backing he would never have gone to England to study law because no merchant of his particular subcaste had ever crossed the black waters before, and the sub-caste elders excommunicated him for being the first to break the caste taboo. Gandhi sailed for England in 1888. When he returned to India, a fully fledged barrister, his mother had died. After an unsuccessful attempt at practising law in India, he took a job in South Africa where he became so involved in social work and in fighting to obtain justice for the Indian community that he eventually settled there. It was during the struggle against General Smuts that he developed the strategy of non-co-operation and passive resistance which was to attract world attention. Gokhale, the great Indian leader, visited him in South Africa and asked him to return to India as his presence was needed there. Therefore, at the beginning of the First World War, Gandhi, his job in South Africa done, returned to India, a hero.

The Gandhi who landed in India in 1915 was a loyal subject of the King-Emperor; a firm believer, like Gokhale himself, that British rule in India was 'an act of Providence'. He declared in a speech to the annual law dinner at Madras soon after his return to India: 'It gives me the greatest pleasure this evening to re-declare my loyalty to the British Empire. I discovered that the British Empire had certain ideals with which I have fallen in love and one of those ideals is that every subject of the British Empire has the freest scope for his energies and honour whatever he thinks is due to his con-science.' However, before long he changed his mind and announced that he could not 'co-operate with evil', and decided to fight the 'Satanic Government'.

What sort of man was Gandhi? Was he a politician, a saint, or as Churchill sniggered, 'a fakir'? These questions have often been asked and are still being asked to this day.

Gandhi was not only the world's leading exponent of non-violence. He was also the greatest social reformer in Indian history. In order to understand him, one has to go back to his youth. The best source on Gandhi is Gandhi himself. His autobiography, *My Experiment with Truth* displays a quite unique honesty.

Gandhi was profoundly influenced by his mother's piety and goodness, by her devotion to the sick and the poor; yet, at the same time he was deeply shocked to discover that so kind-hearted a woman believed that contact with Untouchables was polluting and could forbid him to play with Uka, his Untouchable friend. This perhaps more than anything helped Gandhi to make up his mind to rid India of untouchability; a decision which propelled him into politics and prompted him to want to get rid of the British because, as he kept insisting, 'reform must come from within'. He was of course right. Had the British tried to enforce temple entry for Untouchables, to take only one example, there would have been riots everywhere. The opposition of his caste elders to his going to England to study further confirmed the young man in his belief in the evils of bigotry, but he was too much of a realist to make a frontal attack on caste. Instead, he concentrated his energies on the abolition of untouchability, knowing that for this he could count on the support of the modern-minded and the Western-educated.

Gandhi was not narrow-minded in religious matters, he was a Hindu but even more than a Hindu, he was a theist who, like many good Hindus, held that there are many ways to God. And he had made it a point to learn about other people's religions in order to take for himself the best of their tenets. In his room there used to hang a picture of Christ, and he always began his prayer meetings with Hindu, Muslim and Christian hymns. During his prolonged stay in South Africa, his friends had been mostly either Christians or Muslims; and Gandhi genuinely believed that a man's religion is a personal matter which should not stand in the way of friendship or of joining in a common cause. This belief was to lead him from error to error on his return to India because it made him under-estimate the separateness of the Indian Muslims and their sense of frustration at the prospect of being ruled by a Hindu majority after the departure of the British. When Gandhi kept insisting that he and the Congress Party represented the whole of India, he was sincere; but the mere claim made it certain that the Muslims would in due course demand a state of their own, for they never forgot that they did not look upon the world in the same way as Hindus. Gandhi's sincerity in his belief that Muslims and Hindus were brothers was illustrated when he made his suggestion, at the eleventh hour, that the British should hand India over to a Muslim government rather than divide it. Whether his Congress colleagues would have accepted Gandhi's plan is more doubtful. But his own convictions were finally proved by the test of death. He was murdered by a Hindu fanatic for insisting that the Hindus must give the Muslims their due.

It was in South Africa that Gandhi learnt to run voluntary organizations, to demand and obtain great sacrifices from his followers, to insist that, whatever the provocation, the end never justifies the means. Above all, it was in South Africa that he evolved the technique of passive resistance, and trained a score of devoted disciples who followed him to India. They provided him with the nucleus around which he built up his non-violent army; the army which was to put the British government under increasing pressure to give India her independence.

During his stay abroad, first his three years in England and later his 22 years in South Africa, Gandhi, no longer sheltered by the tentacles of the Hindu joint family, learnt the hard way that people are treated as equals only when they behave as equals, and this lesson he proceeded to teach India.

Three things alienated Gandhi from British rule in India. One was the discovery that after 150 years of 'good government' the Indian peasants were as poor and backward as before, because, he argued, they had become emasculated by foreign rule. Next was the feeling that the British would not go unless forced to go. This feeling was reinforced from time to time by the way in which the government of India always seemed to give too little too late and under pressure. But the key to the whole of Gandhi's attitude to foreign rule was to be found in his dedication to social reform – social reform which for him was the same as truth and God.

Gandhi wanted to cleanse Hinduism of the 'sin of untouch,
ability'; he wanted to bring about equality in all its aspects, not just
equality for Untouchables but equality for women, and equality for
Indians in the eyes of the world. He wanted to bring India back to
the days of Ram Rajya, the Golden Age of Hinduism, when respect
for human beings ranked high, life was simple and villages were
self,sufficient. In order to achieve this, more especially in order to
restore human dignity to the Untouchables and equality to the
women; in order, in the long run, to eradicate caste, he had to get
rid of the British. It was this urge therefore to reform his own society
which, more than anything else, brought him into conflict with the
British people; a people he loved, admired, respected and fought
against for a quarter of a century with extreme courtesy and without
the slightest trace of bitterness. In the course of the struggle he
restored to Indians their self,respect by proving, by his own example,
that one need not be ashamed of material poverty; what really
matters is the wealth of the soul. Gandhi chose to live like the poorest
of the poor, he only travelled third class or on foot, he wore coarse
sandals and the loincloth of the peasant. Because the peasant could
not afford dentures he went about toothless; because the peasant
could not afford good spectacles, he wore the cheapest iron,framed
glasses he could find. When he came to London he went to
Buckingham Palace dressed in his usual way. This was revolu,
tionary at a time when most educated Indians spent much money
and energy on trying to emulate the British.

Like so many social reformers, however, Gandhi was a crank,
and he could be extremely stubborn. He preached sexual abstinence,
even amongst married couples: when his secretary's wife gave birth
to a child, he went on a self,purification fast for having allowed the
couple to take a vow of chastity they were not able to keep. He also
experimented with sex (trying to the end of his life to conquer desire),
with diets, and with nature,cure. His fads extended to regarding tea
as Westerners do pep,pills. He indulged in fasting as a form of political
blackmail, and defended himself with the argument that his fasts were
the same kind of coercion which Christ exercised from the cross.

He harried the British with his speeches, his articles, his fasts, his

uncanny gift for symbolism which led him to make salt from sea-
water in breach of the government monopoly, as a challenge to the
government's authority, and to insist on all his followers spending
some time every day in hand-spinning, as a sign of their real concern
for the villager's poverty. He wormed concession after concession
out of the government yet he never departed from his insistence on
peaceful means and the importance of human dignity. He claimed
to be one of the masses; and in order to reach the masses he had to
talk to them in words they would understand, he had to appeal to
their hearts. Since the majority of the mass was Hindu, and because
he was so concerned with reforming Hinduism, he often spoke in
Hindu terms. In the process he alienated the Muslims who saw no
place for themselves in Gandhi's India, despite all his protestations
that Hindus and Muslims were brothers. Pakistan in fact has two
Hindu and two Muslim progenitors: Gandhi and Nehru, Sir
Sayyid Ahmed Khan and Mohamed Ali Jinnah.

It was the Rowlatt Acts which brought Gandhi into open
opposition to British rule in India. He objected to the arbitrariness
of the Acts, and called for non-co-operation. In response to his call,
many Indians resigned from office and returned their decorations.
Students boycotted the universities. Congressmen picketed liquor
and foreign cloth shops. Of more doubtful wisdom was the Congress boycott of the first elections on an enlarged franchise under the
1919 Act. From that time onward, the Western educated in India
divided between those who, following Gandhi, stayed in opposition
till Independence, and those who co-operated with the British
because of their belief that any future Indian rulers would need to be
trained in modern skills. As time went on, a gulf was thus created
between India's government servants and India's politicians.

Gandhi's appeal for non-co-operation stirred Indian imagination
as nothing had done previously. Thanks to the English language,
now widely spoken by the educated; thanks to the English-language
newspapers published all over India; thanks to modern means of
communication; Gandhi's appeal was carried across linguistic
boundaries. This created, for the first time in Indian history, a
nationalism which was not confined to one group, one region or one

language, but which went deep amongst the people, and made people in Bengal and Bombay, in Madras and Gujerat, feel Indians together. Gandhi had an extraordinary flare for publicity and an uncanny gift for harassing his opponents. From 1919 onwards he gave the British government in India no rest and even when he was in jail he was a source of embarrassment; a 'gadfly'.

In 1922 Gandhi was tried for the first time and sentenced to six years imprisonment for sedition. He had written articles preaching disaffection to the government. He had intended the disaffection to be non-violent, but an excited mob in a remote village set fire to the police station and policemen were burnt to death. Gandhi called off the boycott, admitted to a 'Himalayan blunder', pleaded guilty and willingly went to jail. The trial is so typical of the tone he set on Indo-British relations that it is worth reporting at some length for it goes a long way in explaining the unique lack of bitterness which characterizes these relations.

After the Advocate General had stated the case against Gandhi, the Judge asked if he had anything to say. Gandhi read out the following statement:

The Advocate General was entirely fair. . . . It is very true that I have no desire whatsoever to conceal from this Court the fact that to preach disaffection towards the existing system of government has become almost a passion with me. . . . I do not ask for mercy. I do not plead any extenuating act. I am here . . . to invite and cheerfully submit to the highest penalty that can be inflicted upon me for what in law is a deliberate crime and what appears to me to be the highest duty of a citizen. The only course open to you, the Judge, is, as I am going to say . . . either to resign your post, or inflict on me the severest penalty if you believe that the system and the law you administer are good for the people. I do not expect that kind of conversion, but by the time I have finished with my statement you will perhaps have a glimpse of what is raging within my breast to run this maddest risk that a man can run. (I want to) explain why, from a staunch loyalist and co-operator, I have become an uncompromising disaffectionist and non-co-operator. . . . I came reluctantly to the conclusion that the

67

British connection had made India more helpless than she ever was before, politically and economically. . . . She has become so (helpless) that she has little power of resisting famines. Before the British advent, India spun and wove in her millions of cottages just the supplement she needed for adding to her meagre agricultural resources. This cottage industry, so vital for India's existence, has been ruined by incredibly heartless and inhuman processes as described by English witnesses. Little do town dwellers know how the semi-starved masses of India are slowly sinking to lifelessness. . . . No sophistry, no jugglery in figures, can explain away the evidence that the skeletons in many villages present to the naked eye. I have no doubt that both England and the town-dwellers of India will have to answer, if there is a God above, for this crime against humanity which is perhaps unequalled in history. . . . I am satisfied that many Englishmen and Indian officials honestly believe that they are administering one of the best systems devised in the world and that India is making steady though slow progress. They do not know that a subtle but effective system of terrorism and an organized display of force on the one hand, and the deprivation of all powers of retaliation and self-defence on the other, have emasculated the people and induced in them the habit of simulation. This awful habit has added to the ignorance and self-deception of the administrators. . . . I have no personal ill will against any administrator, much less have I disaffection towards the King's person. But I hold it an honour to be disaffected towards a government which in its totality has done more harm to India than any previous system. India is less manly under the British rule than she ever was before . . . it has been a precious privilege for me to be able to write what I have in the various articles tendered in evidence against me. . . . In my opinion, non-co-operation with evil is as much a duty as is co-operation with good.

And before he sat down he asked the Judge for the maximum sentence. The judge, later Mr Justice Broomfield, bowed to Gandhi and said:

The determination of a just sentence is perhaps as difficult a proposition as a judge in this country could have to face. The law is no respecter of persons. Nevertheless, it will be impossible to ignore the fact that you are in a different category from any person I have ever tried or am likely to have to try. It would be impossible to ignore the fact that, in the eyes of millions of your countrymen, you are a great patriot and a great leader. Even those who differ from you in politics look upon you as a man of high ideals and of noble and even saintly life.

Then Mr Broomfield sentenced him to six years' imprisonment adding that if government reduced the sentence 'no one would be better pleased than I'. Gandhi thanked the Judge for a sentence 'as mild as any Judge could inflict on me, and so far as the entire proceedings are concerned, I must say that I could not have expected greater courtesy'.

It is because of dialogues such as these; dialogues never allowed to degenerate into recrimination or abuse, that Britain and India could glide into the friendliest of partnerships at Independence. The main beneficiary was India which slipped from Colonial to Common, wealth status without disruption, and the credit for this smooth transition which has provided free India with a firm basis for nationhood goes first to Mahatma Gandhi, to his insistence on eschewing violence; and next to the British government for its patience and to the many Britons in India and in Britain for their understanding support for what Gandhi was trying to achieve.

Gandhi kept the British on the run. In 1928 they sent out the Simon Commission to study at first hand conditions for granting Dominion Status to India, but they made one error; they did not include an Indian. Gandhi therefore called for a boycott of the Commission. The Simon Commission spent a year in India, and despite the Congress boycott it produced an excellent report and made recom, mendations which were to provide the basis for the 1935 Act. However, the boycott had its success too; never again did the British exclude Indians from their proceedings. Another indirect result of the Commission's visit to India was the decision of Clement

Attlee, one of its members, that an unwilling India was more than it would be worth for Britain to hold. The moment Attlee became Prime Minister, 18 years later, he pulled Britain out of India, putting into effect Ramsay MacDonald's deferred hope that 'within a period of months, rather than years, there will be a new dominion added to the Commonwealth of our Nations, a dominion which will find self-respect as an equal within the Commonwealth'.

The Simon Commission was followed by two Round Table Conferences in London. Both these Conferences failed to reach agreement; the first because Congress was not represented, the second because Gandhi – the sole Congress nominee – insisted that Congress represented the whole of India; a contention which not only Mr Jinnah and Dr Ambedkar (the Untouchable leader) but also the Indian princes were not prepared to accept. While it is true that both Conferences failed, they were useful in showing to the British government the background against which it would have to hand over power.

In 1934 Gandhi resigned from the Congress Party and devoted himself to social reform and village uplift. However, the Congress leaders he had trained depended heavily upon him for advice until after Independence.

The Second Round Table Conference was followed by the 1935 Government of India Act. This roused much hostility from the right-wing Tories led by Churchill who saw that from the 1935 Act to Independence there was only a short step. The Act laid down the framework for a Federal government of India; with provinces no longer under the control of the government of India for their own subjects, an expanded electorate, and elected ministers responsible for all departments. The minorities – Muslims, Untouchables, Anglo-Indians and Britons – were given special seats to protect their interests. Provision was also made for the princes to accede for certain subjects to a Central government, to which they would send their nominated members and the provinces their elected members. The Viceroy was to keep control of defence and foreign affairs. The Governors of the provinces and the Viceroy were given certain special powers to protect government servants; to see that law and order and financial solvency were maintained; and, in extreme circumstances, to suspend the elected governments.

The 1935 Government of India Act was put into effect in 1937. As a result of the elections which were then held, the Congress Party won power everywhere in what is now India, except in Assam and Bengal which had large Muslim populations. They also lost power in what is now Pakistan with the exception of the North West Frontier Province. After some argument with the Viceroy about the powers reserved for the Provincial Governors, the elected Ministries took office and they ruled for two years, gaining invaluable administrative experience. But when Britain's entry into the Second World War automatically involved India as well, without con sultation, the Congress Ministers resigned in protest. Congress sympathies were with Britain, but to be implicated in war without consultation seemed intolerable. The non Congress Ministers – in the main in what is now Pakistan – however, did not resign, earning for themselves a gratitude in Britain which was to stand them in good stead in the future.

The provisions of the 1935 Act for a united India failed for two reasons. First, the princes, who could not agree as to who should represent them, stayed out. Secondly, the Congress walk out in 1939 left the Muslim League a free field to make propaganda for Pakistan. When India was divided, it was a severe blow to British interests. Instead of an ally capable of playing Britain's role in the heart of Asia and keeping law and order in the Indian Ocean, she had two states whose strength was wasted in their quarrels with each other.

In the last few years of British rule everybody lost except the Muslim League. Britain lost the chance of a united India able to take over the role she had played in Asia for over a century. The princes' refusal to co operate lost them their only chance of playing the balancing part in Indian politics which might have saved them from extinction. But the worst loss of all was that Congress missed the last chance it had of obtaining a united independent India. This was largely Nehru's doing when in 1937 he refused to agree to a coalition government for his native United Provinces. Nehru insisted on the two Muslim Ministers being members of the Congress

Party rather than of the Muslim League. This insistence confirmed many Indian Muslims in their fear that they would never get a fair deal from Hindus once the British left. It was this sharpening of suspicion which gave Jinnah and the Muslim League their chance. Jinnah, an ex-Congressman, had retired from politics to practise law in London. He now returned to India and took over the Muslim League, hitherto a weak party, and turned it into a formid-able opponent of the Congress. In 1940 he began to demand the creation of Pakistan; in 1947 he got it.

Just as the First World War had given the Indian economy great opportunities for development so the Second World War gave such impetus to development and Indianization that it made Indepen-dence possible, even in conservative eyes. The armed forces were expanded; for the first time Indians became officers on a very large scale and hundreds of thousands of Indian soldiers were trained in new skills; and a small air force and navy were created. Above all, the manifold activities of a government and an economy at war gave a quite new scope for responsibility to the Indian middle classes and with new responsibilities comes new self-respect. Now that many Indians were doing things only a few had been doing before, and doing them well, they no longer saw any reason for the continuance of British rule. They proved to their own satisfaction, and indeed to the satisfaction of the foreign ruler himself, that they were efficient not only as soldiers and administrators but also as industrialists and technicians. A new prosperity swept over the countryside as inflation raised the price of food grains and made it possible for the peasants to pay off their debts to the moneylenders.

The time seemed auspicious for co-operation and Whitehall was quick to sense the opportunity. Sir Stafford Cripps went specially to India in 1942 in order to offer the Congress all it had been asking for except Defence, and to promise Independence immediately after the war. But Gandhi did not trust the British not to go back on their word after the war, and he was also worried by the Japanese advance in Southeast Asia. He felt that he was now in a position to bargain for the whole and made his second fundamental political mistake when he turned down Cripps' offer as a 'post-dated cheque'.

Gandhi's rejection of the Cripps offer was the last nail in the coffin of Indian unity for it destroyed the last possibility of co-operation between the Congress and the Muslim League. The League, it will be remembered, unlike the Congress, was backing the war effort. Had Gandhi accepted Cripps' offer it is just possible that wartime co-operation between the Congress and the League might have been extended to co-operation in a federal undivided India after Independence. However, the opportunity was missed and, to make matters worse, no sooner had Cripps returned to Britain than Gandhi launched his 'Quit India' movement. Gandhi wanted the movement to remain peaceful, but when the British government, at this most difficult moment of the war put all the Congress leaders in jail, there was a flare-up of violence; trains were derailed, bridges were blown up, and for the first time real bitterness crept into Anglo-Indian relations, giving the Muslim League its opportunity to win British hearts.

In 1943, famine broke out in Bengal, where communications had been disrupted by the war and where maladministration under a mainly Muslim ministry was rife. The Viceroy, reluctant to super-sede an elected and co-operating provincial government, hesitated to interfere. Three million people died of hunger in Bengal. By the time the Central government did interfere many people were beyond saving. This failure of trusteeship, added to the failure of British rule to protect Burma and Malaya from Japanese aggression, finally destroyed Britain's hold on the Indian educated middle classes – the only ones which mattered since the masses could not be stirred *in favour* of Britain staying on – so that by 1945 everybody was waiting for the end of the British Empire in India. The Indians were impatient to rule themselves. The British were exhausted by the war and the Labour government was anxious to lay down an imperial burden it had always seen as a preparation for the earliest possible self-government. The Muslim League which did by now represent most of India's Muslims was clamouring for Pakistan while the Congress which represented practically everybody else was clamour-ing for Independence at all cost and *now*.

The only problem facing Britain was to whom to hand over

power. Should she simply walk out (as she did in Palestine in 1948) and let the Indians fight it out between themselves, Hindus, Muslims, princes, leaving the erstwhile jewel prey to chaos and civil war? Such a course of action was unthinkable; no self-respecting imperial government could contemplate such irresponsibility and destroy the century and a half of consolidation and construction in India of which Britain was so justly proud. Should Britain force a Hindu–Muslim coalition and hand power over to a united federal central government? Britain put forward this solution and sent out a Cabinet Mission, headed by Cripps, for the purpose. But the Cabinet Mission failed to obtain co-operation first from the Muslim League then from the Congress; and the princes who were too busy counting their gun salutes to read the writing on the wall did not use their collective bargaining power. The Cabinet Mission went away bitterly disappointed, but not without committing Britain in the event of a withdrawal, to the announcement that paramountcy would lapse; an announcement which was to have serious consequences both for the Indian princes themselves and for the successor states of India and Pakistan. After the failure of the Cabinet Mission, the only solution left to the British government was to divide and quit.

This Attlee proceeded to do without undue delay. It has already been mentioned that during his visit to India as secretary of the Simon Commission he had come to the conclusion that it was not worth trying to keep an unwilling India. Now he was further pushed into speedy action by two factors no Prime Minister could ignore. At home in Britain the electorate was tired of keeping the peace for the world. No government could have survived which argued that conscripts should be sent to India by the hundreds of thousands for an undetermined period of time in order that Indian Independence be delayed by a few years for the sake of a more orderly transfer of power. If Britain had tried to stay on in India for another few years, it might well have created a Cyprus-terrorist situation on a giant scale. Equally important in helping Attlee to make up his mind not to waste a minute were developments in India.

No sooner had the Cabinet Mission left Indian soil than Jinnah

74

called for 15 August to be observed as a Direct Action Day. How he intended this Direct Action Day to take shape besides holding prayers and taking out processions, was not very clear. Whatever he had intended, his wording was sufficiently violent for the Muslim Chief Minister of Bengal to interpret it as a call to Jehad, war against the infidel, and to organize a huge anti-Hindu riot. For the first couple of days the Hindus were too stunned to retaliate, then they struck back. By the end of Direct Action which lasted nearly a week, 16,000 people had been killed and a communal frenzy hitherto unknown had been let loose across India. In Calcutta more Muslims had been killed than Hindus, so the Muslims of East Bengal retaliated by killing Hindus and – much more serious than murder – raping women. Then in Bihar, to avenge the East Bengal Hindus, Muslims were killed, and the madness spread north to the Frontier and the Punjab. The British were no longer able to keep order; their last justification to rule India had gone.

Gandhi, who had retired from politics, was heartbroken. All his life he had preached non-violence and brotherly love. As the independence for which he had fought for so long drew closer it began to seem hardly worth having, for it looked as if it would be not independence but death that the British would leave behind. Gandhi was essentially a man of action; what the Hindus call a Karma Yoga. Despite his great age and his poor health, he at once announced that he would only eat half as much as was required to keep himself alive, and that he would walk through Bengal to restore sanity and confidence amongst the affected villagers. He walked for months in East Bengal on a 500-calorie diet – his half-fast unto death. So great was his influence with the common people that he managed to bring back peace, at least to East Bengal. But Gandhi could not be everywhere at once, and riots of unprecedented ferocity broke out in Bihar and the Punjab. To suppress, let alone to prevent them, would have required far more British troops than were available. So, on 20 February 1947 Clement Attlee announced that the British would leave India, come what may, and he named June 1948 as the leaving date. To liquidate the Empire, he sent out

Queen Victoria's grandson, Lord Louis Mountbatten, with the following instructions:

It is the definite objective of His Majesty's Government to obtain a unitary government for British India and the Indian states, if possible within the British Commonwealth, through the medium of a Constituent Assembly, set up and run in accordance with the Cabinet Mission's plan, and you should do the utmost in your power to persuade all parties to work together to this end, and advise His Majesty's Government, in the light of developments, as to the steps that will have to be taken.

Since, however, this plan cannot become operative in respect of British India by agreement between the major parties, there can be no question of compelling either major party to accept it. . . .

It is, of course, important that the Indian states should adjust their relations with the authorities to whom it is intended to hand over power in British India; but as was explicitly stated by the Cabinet Mission, His Majesty's Government do not intend to hand over their powers and obligations under paramountcy to any successor government. It is not intended to bring paramountcy as a system to a conclusion earlier than the date of the final transfer of power, but you are authorized, at such time as you think appropriate, to enter into negotiations with individual states for adjusting their relations with the Crown.

You will do your best to persuade the rulers of any Indian states in which political progress has been slow. . . . You will also aid and assist the states in coming to fair and just arrangements with the leaders of British India as to their future relationships.

The date fixed for the transfer of power is a flexible one to within one month; but you should aim at 1 June 1948 as the effective date for the transfer of power. . . .

You should take every opportunity of stressing the importance of ensuring that the transfer of power is effected with full regard to the defence requirements of India. In the first place you will impress upon the Indian leaders the great importance of avoiding any breach in the continuity of the Indian Army and of maintaining the organization of defence upon an all-Indian basis. . . .

76

By the time Mountbatten landed in Delhi tension had reached such a pitch, politicians were so divided and the administration had become so paralysed that it had become clear that delay would only mean more tension and administrative disintegration. If Britain was to hand over power in working order there was no time to lose. Mountbatten advised Attlee to bring forward the dateline and to announce that the British would leave India on the 15 August 1947, six months away. The justification for what the Tories denounced as 'indecent haste' was the correct appreciation that only the shock of realizing that time was running out could make Congress and Muslim League leaders agree to sit at the same table to discuss the manner of the transfer of power, instead of shadow-boxing. And having failed to get the leaders to agree to hand over power to a united India, Mountbatten produced a blueprint for division which was accepted by the Congress and the Muslim League.[1]

The blueprint provided that the part of British India which had a Muslim majority would form the state of Pakistan if its people so wished; that the part of British India which had a non-Muslim majority would form the new India. Therefore Pakistan would consist of the North West Frontier Province, Baluchistan, the western half of the Punjab which was to be divided on religious lines, Sind, and East Bengal. However, since East Bengal is a thousand miles away from the other provinces which were to make up Pakistan, this meant that there would in fact be two Pakistans: East Pakistan and West Pakistan connected to each other only by air or sea.

As far as the princely states were concerned Mountbatten's hands had been tied from the start. There was Cripps' announcement that paramountcy – the special treaty relationship between the princes and the British Crown which was ratified after the Mutiny – would lapse. Even more important there was the widespread Tory feeling that Britain owed a debt of honour to its faithful allies, and a step as important as giving India Independence, had the Labour govern-ment not carried the Tories with it, would have divided the nation. Therefore the rational solution was not open to Mountbatten. This rational solution, the one which would have in fact been fairest to all parties concerned, including the princes, would have been to say that the successor states (India and Pakistan) would inherit the paramountcy of the princely states according to geographical propinquity and religious composition. Had this been done there would have been no problems over Kashmir, Hyderabad or Junagadh, and relations between India and Pakistan might not have been as bad as they are.

To avoid trouble, Mountbatten advised the princes that it would be in their interest to accede to either India or Pakistan according to the geographical location of their state and to the religion of its people. Thus Jaisalmer, with a Hindu population and contiguous to both countries, should accede to India; while Bahawalpur also contiguous to both countries but with a Muslim population, should accede to Pakistan. Unfortunately Mountbatten's advice was not mandatory and not all the princes were clear sighted enough to make the right choice. Trouble began when Junagadh, a state with a Muslim ruler but a Hindu population and without contact with Pakistan except by sea, acceded to Pakistan. Jinnah, hoping to bargain with India, accepted this accession although he had himself stated that he agreed with Mountbatten's formula (probably with Kashmir in mind). The people of Junagadh rose against their ruler, India sent troops to the border of the state, the ruler fled to Pakistan and his Muslim Prime Minister acceded to India. The last state to give trouble was the biggest of them all: Hyderabad, which is landlocked in India. The Muslim Nizam of Hyderabad, who ruled over a mainly Hindu population, decided to remain independent since he could not join Pakistan. The Nizam signed a standstill agreement with India but broke it by importing arms from Pakistan by air. A swift police action in 1948 gave Hyderabad to India to the anger of Pakistan which had been hoping to trade Hyderabad against Kashmir. Of the three problem states, Junagadh and Hyderabad indeed no longer exist; according to the wishes of their people they have been absorbed into the surrounding linguistic groups during the linguistic reorganization of India. Only Kashmir remains a festering thorn in the IndoPakistani side, a great source of embarrassment to Britain, and a threat to peace in Asia.

The worst trouble was over Kashmir. Kashmir, a Muslim majority state, had a Hindu ruler. Mountbatten did his best to persuade him to make his mind up before the date of the transfer of power; he told the Maharajah that India would not object if he acceded to Pakistan, so long as the politicians in Kashmir agreed; and if he wanted to accede to India that too would be all right so long as he did it while the British were still in power and could underwrite his choice – Kashmir stands for the K in Pakistan, so it was realized there might be trouble. But the Maharajah dithered on after Independence and Muslim tribesmen invaded his state with the connivance of Pakistan. The Maharajah asked India to help. Mountbatten, who had by then become Governor-General of India, advised the Indian Prime Minister to demand Kashmir's accession before sending troops to the state's rescue in order to make inter- vention legal. Pakistan had lost its legal claim to Kashmir especially since Jinnah had stated that the decision of the ruler would be final; but since the majority of the people of Kashmir are Muslims, Pakistan continues to feel that it has a moral claim to the state. The result is that ever since then India and Pakistan have been facing each other in a static war under the supervision of UN observers while the Kashmir question remains unsolved before the Security Council, blocked by a Soviet veto.

However, the problems created by the irresponsibility of these three Indian princes pale into insignificance compared to the holo- caust which followed Partition. The killings were largely confined to the Punjab and to Delhi thanks to the determination of the Chief Minister of the United Provinces who used massive force to protect his Muslims and closed his border to Hindu refugees. In the Punjab there was a complete breakdown of law and order, and perhaps 300,000 people were killed while in a couple of months 11 million people migrated searching for security in the greatest exodus of history. Mountbatten's mixed Boundary Force of 55,000 men under British command stood almost helpless while loot, arson and murder swept the land. In Bengal, by contrast, thanks to Gandhi's presence, there was no trouble. Gandhi, who had anticipated that in view of the past year's communal rioting the trouble would be

79

worst in Bengal had gone to Calcutta where he walked from house to house in the company of the Muslim Chief Minister preaching Hindu-Muslim brotherliness. So great was the confidence he inspired that nobody ran away or got killed – the running away took place three years later when three million Hindus fled from a Pakistan which treated them like second-class citizens. Mountbatten, filled with admiration, called Gandhi a 'one man boundary force', who could succeed where 55,000 soldiers had failed.

Soon after Independence Gandhi was shot by a fanatic Hindu because he insisted that India should treat Pakistan fairly and hand over its share of the gold reserves of undivided India, even while the two countries were at war in Kashmir.

Gandhi's life had been devoted to the attainment of truth and goodness; to the eradication of social evils within his own society; and to the restoration of India's self respect. He never quite achieved the sainthood for which he strove so hard, but after his death some of the social reforms which mattered most to him, the legal emanci-pation of women and Untouchables were put into effect. Moreover, he provided India with many of the leaders who were to make Independence successful, for his greatest gift was the capacity to pick and train men for the jobs which lay ahead.

19 The Dutch began trading with India in the seventeenth century. A seventeenth-century engraving of the office of the Dutch East India Company at Pulicat.

20 The British and French were among the contenders for control of India and their relations eventually deteriorated into the Seven Years War (1756–63). An eighteenth-century plan of the British attack on Geriah Fort dates from this period.

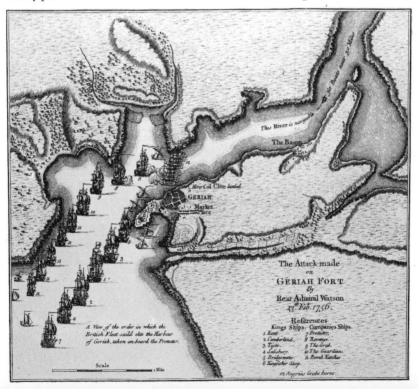

21 The Portuguese navigator Vasco da Gama (c. 1460–1524) had created trade with India as early as 1498. A seventeenth-century engraving.

22 When he landed at Calicut he was received by the Zamorin or ruler. A nineteenth-century engraving based on a painting by Smythe.

23 This map drawn in the early eighteenth century shows India as she appeared to a traveller of the period.

A General Map of India Intra Ganges

Bengall

Hughly R.

Piply

Balasore

Cambay

Baroach

Suratt

Damaan

C. S. John

Tarapore

Bussaim

Bombay

Chaul

Dunde Rajah pouri

Dabull

Cape Z.

Sangueseer

Rajah pouri

Ghiria

Vingurla

Goa

Carwarr

Merjee

Ounoar

Bataela

Barsalore

Mangalore

Decullu

Mount Delly

Cannanore

Tellichery

Burgura

Callicutt

Tannore

Penany

Chitua

Granganore

Couchin

St. Andrea

Porca

Coiloan

Anjenga

Tegna patam

Decann

Cuncan

Vizapore

Cann-ara

Mallabarr

Marjour

Mall a barr

Cape Comorr

Part of the Laccadivas

Quallipenny

Hanimandow

Maldiva

The Kings Island

Islands

Raposta

Adaman

Morjour

Manypaar

Hitacorn a barr

Coili

Adam Bridge

Panat Pedro

Negapatan

Tranquinbar

Porto Nova

Fort St. David

Pando Cherry

St. Thomas

Fort St. George

Seaven Pagodos

Paleacate

Krisna patam

Pettapolly

Chormendell

Carango

Maduk patam

Raud

Matura

Vizoga Patam

Bimli Patam

Calinga Patam

Borrum

Suraopore

Gonjam

Maniltha

Jugurnat

Ashipur

Raisor

Orixa

Golcondah

Palicate

ZELOAN

Jaffnapatam

Callpatego

Tranq. Maliga

Baddula

Negomba

Colombo

Barbarin

P. de Galle

Mattura

Dunder Point

Little Abaxios

Great Abaxios

Ro. Mylne sc.

24 An eighteenth-century engraving of Surat where one of the British East India Company's first factories was established in 1612.

25 The extension of British power involved conflict with the Marathas and the Sultan Tipu of Mysore. A nineteenth-century engraving of the assault of Seringapatam in 1788 when the Sultan was defeated.

26 The British army consisted mainly of natives or Sepoys. A nineteenth-century engraving of a Sepoy.

27 This engraving dating from the same period illustrates the British assault of Delhi in 1857 caused by the mutiny among the native troops.

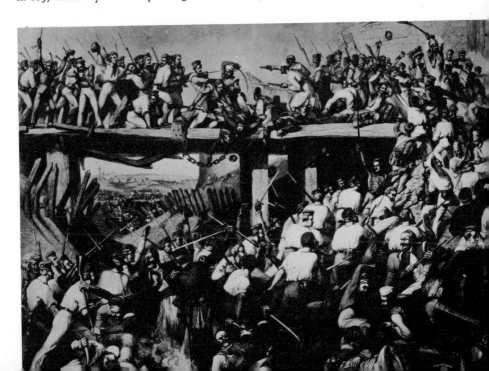

28 Robert Clive (1725–74) by increasing the power of the Company is recognized as the founder of the Empire of British India. From an engraving after a painting by Reynolds.

29 Warren Hastings (1732–1818) was the first Governor-General of British India. He was accused of peculation in 1786 and at his trial seen here was acquitted. An eighteenth-century engraving.

30 The British families who settled in India preserved their habits and customs. A nineteenth-century engraving.

31 Contact between Britons and Indians became confined to the requirements of administration and domesticity. A nineteenth-century photograph of a British officer being carried in a palanquin.

32 Some of the Indian customs were regarded with cynicism by the British. A nineteenth-century cartoon illustrating suttee – the burning of the wife on her husband's funeral pyre.

33 Although suttee is no longer practised the Hindu custom of burning the dead is still preserved.

4   Independence

AT INDEPENDENCE India was led by two men, Patel and
Nehru; as far apart and antipathetic as the poles, yet complementary,
shackled to each other by Gandhi, who on the day of his death,
made the older, abler and wiser man promise that he would support
the volatile and charismatic Nehru as long as he lived. Gandhi, who
had a premonition of his death, wanted to help consolidate India's
new-won freedom and he knew that left to themselves the two men
would compete for power.

Pandit Jawaharlal Nehru, India's first Prime Minister, was the son
of an extremely talented, self-made and slightly *nouveau riche* lawyer-
politician from Allahabad. He was educated at Harrow and
Cambridge. On his return to India he tried his hand at the bar
without much success. Fired by Gandhi's call for non-co-operation,
Nehru was arrested in 1922. Before going to jail he read out the
following statement:

> Less than 10 years ago, I returned from England after a long stay
> there. . . . I had imbibed most of the prejudices of Harrow and
> Cambridge, and in my likes and dislikes I was perhaps more an
> Englishman than an Indian. I looked upon the world almost
> from an Englishman's standpoint . . . as much prejudiced in
> favour of England and the English as it was possible for an Indian
> to be.

Nehru looked at the world through the eyes of the Fabian socialist
he, like so many of his contemporaries, had become, largely as a
reaction to his father's Edwardian way of life and extreme angliciza-
tion. Indeed, the younger Nehru became more and more attracted

89

by communism; after a four-day visit to Soviet Russia in 1927 he wrote: 'Whatever its faults, communism is not hypocritical and not imperialistic' and on his return to India he presided over a Republican Conference and tried to move the Congress at its annual session into accepting a socialist anti-imperialist policy. Gandhi, who had been keeping careful watch on the young man was so profoundly shocked that he wrote to protest: 'You are going too fast. The differences between us are so vast and radical that there seems to be no meeting ground between us.' Yet Gandhi decided to capture Nehru by making him Congress President instead of letting him break away and lead a leftist party.

There were two reasons for Gandhi's decision. First, he knew that Nehru was an appeaser at heart and that if he were put in charge of the Congress he would always follow the majority rather than stand on his own. The second reason was that Gandhi instinctively agreed with Nehru's father who had written:

> The revolt of youth has become an accomplished fact . . . the need of the hour is the head of Gandhi and the voice of Jawahar. . . . There are strong reasons for either you or Jawahar to wear the 'Crown' (the presidentship of the Congress) and if you . . . stand together . . . it does not really matter who it is that stands in front and who behind.

Gandhi knew the only way he could control Nehru was by making him stand in front. He did this without wasting time, with the result that Nehru was always the captive of the Congress; talking left, acting middle of the road.

As far as Nehru was concerned, there was little in Gandhi's approach and programme with which he agreed, but he instinctively knew that 'Gandhi was India' and that this identification made it impossible for anyone to move the Indian masses without his support. Nehru wanted to mobilize the masses and he therefore needed Gandhi's support. In addition there was personal attraction (that sympathy Gandhi was such a master at generating), a shared concern for the poor and the backward, a common repulsion for the use of force, and a common love for India.

Between Gandhi and Nehru a marriage of convenience was thus evolved: no matter how much the two disagreed – and their views differed on almost everything – they dared not risk a divorce which might upset India. Gandhi wanted to do away with industrializa- tion to concentrate on handicrafts and self-sufficient villages; he wanted to replace textile mills by handspinning; he insisted on prohibition and abstinence. But his primary concern was the abolition of untouchability and the reform of Hinduism in its social aspects. Nehru liked sherry, believed in family planning and was unscathed by the bigotry of Hinduism, ignorant of social con- ditions in the villages. His primary concern was with socialism, industrialization, scientific progress, planning, bringing India from what he used to call the 'cowdung age' into the atomic age. Had India been independent when both men were still in their prime, there would have had to be a divorce. Gandhi's timely death made it possible for Nehru to go as far on the road of his choice as the Congress backbenchers would let him. Many things have therefore been done for India's good in Gandhi's name of which he would not have approved.

Next to Nehru, far abler, yet deliberately playing a subordinate part, was Sardar Patel. He was India's Deputy Prime Minister and Gandhi's right-hand man. An administrator of genius and a man of decision, he had all the qualities Nehru lacked. India owes a great deal to Sardar Patel for the manner in which he solved the problems with which India was faced at Independence; from the reconciliation of the services and the politicians to the integration of the princely states. Unfortunately for India, Sardar Patel died two years after Gandhi. Nehru, no administrator and no delegator of authority, was therefore left alone to tackle the administrative problems of unifying and modernizing India.

In addition to Sardar Patel and Nehru, there were the Congress politicians, many of whom had learnt to govern during the short period of office when Congress was co-operating with the govern- ment; many of them had been handpicked by Gandhi and trained by Patel. Then there were the Indian members of the Indian Civil Service; some 350 experienced and dedicated administrators upon whose shoulders fell the brunt of the job of running India. The subordinate services were already fully Indianized and the Indian army which had been tested in war had by now some 5,000 Indian officers, though only a handful of really senior ones.

In 1947 the Congress Party was immensely popular, despite the trauma of Partition. It carried the halo of having won Independence and the villagers looked on its leaders as national heroes.

When the Indian tricolour was unfurled to the booming of guns on 15 August 1947 there was great rejoicing in India; but the rejoicing was short-lived, for within hours the new state had to face reality.

Some of the problems of Partition had to be solved at once. The most pressing which could not wait was the problem of the rehabilitation of the refugees. Over six million people poured into the Indian Punjab, with as much of their moveable property as they had managed to take away in their hasty flight to safety. They had left behind their bank accounts, their fertile canal-irrigated colonies and their homes. To make the problem of their rehabilitation more difficult, the land vacated in India by the Muslims who had fled to Pakistan was often un-irrigated, and the Muslims who had left were much poorer than the newcomers. The result was that it was impossible to give the refugees land and homes in any way equivalent to those they had left behind. There was much bitterness at Pakistan's refusal to pay compensation for the difference in value of evacuee property or to let the refugees return to Pakistan to collect their belongings and liquidate their assets. However, within a very few years the refugee problem was solved in northern India; partly by the refugees' acceptance of a reduction in their standard of living, partly by government grants, but largely by the initiative of the hardy Punjabi peasants themselves, who are amongst India's most enterprising farmers. Eventually, too, their rehabilitation has been helped by the construction of the Bhakra Dam which irrigates over $3\frac{1}{2}$ million acres of land, and by the creation of the new city of Chandigarh, designed by Le Corbusier as the capital of the Indian Punjab; the old capital of the undivided Punjab, Lahore, went to Pakistan.

While the rehabilitation of the refugees in northern India was relatively easy, in West Bengal by contrast the situation is, to this day, very far from satisfactory. At the time of Partition, because of Gandhi's presence in Bengal, no massacres and no exchange of population took place there as it did in the north. Some 13 million Hindus remained in East Pakistan, but by 1950 much of the Hindu *élite* had migrated to Calcutta. There were many reasons for this migration: from the attraction of the big city to the fact that Hindus were being deliberately discriminated against in Pakistan. They were refused jobs, deprived of proper political representations by the unwelcome provision of separate electorates, and of their economic status by drastic land reforms confined to East Pakistan where the Muslims were mostly the tenants in contrast to West Pakistan where they were also the landlords. By 1950 over a million and a half refugees had migrated to Calcutta, but they had come gradually and their presence had gone unnoticed; they had found jobs and homes for themselves with the help of relations who had been living in Calcutta for generations. Suddenly in 1950 hundreds of thousands of terrified refugees poured into Calcutta and the problem became acute. In all, by the end of 1950, three and a half million Hindus had fled to India from East Pakistan for safety because they were being treated as second-class citizens; because they were harassed; because there had been riots in which women had been abducted and people killed; but above all because, deprived of leadership, they were afraid. These new refugees were very difficult to rehabilitate; the *élite* which had preceded them had bought-up all the spare land of Bengal, and crowded into every nook and corner of Calcutta leaving no accommodation empty; and since the Muslims of West Bengal were not migrating to Pakistan on the same scale there was literally nowhere to put the refugees. Consequently they had to squat in camps little better than concentration camps and live on government doles. In the end, the government of India tried to reclaim a large area from the jungle in central India in order to rehabilitate them but without much success. Many Bengali refugees were unenterprising, incompetent and disheartened. They were not prepared to fend for themselves; they simply ran back to Calcutta to beg, steal and swell the mob of agitators which makes the second largest city in the British Commonwealth such an unpleasant place. What happened in 1950 happened again in 1964 when communal riots flared up first in East Bengal, followed by riots in West Bengal, followed again by riots in Dacca – the capital of East Pakistan – in which at least 1,000 Hindus were killed, followed yet again by riots in central India in which many Muslims were killed. With each communal riot more Hindus leave East Pakistan for good adding to the congestion of Calcutta and the surrounding country side, bringing fresh bitterness with them to poison Indo Pakistani relations, and reminding the Muslims in India that they are a minority whose security can at any time be threatened by the behaviour of the authorities in Pakistan.

Another problem resulting from Partition is the fate of Kashmir which has been put in cold storage. Pakistan claims that the people of Kashmir should be given a chance to express their wishes and decide whether they want to join India or Pakistan. India claims that Kashmir is legally part of India, that the people made their choice clear on three occasions by electing a government in favour of accession to India. The accession of Kashmir to India was fully in accordance with law. However, India had not yet fulfilled the promise it made at the time of accession to hold a plebiscite, and the Indian argument that the election results represent the people's verdict is somewhat invalidated by the fact that Sheikh Abdullah, the Kashmiri leader, was kept in jail for 11 years pending trial because he wanted Kashmir to be independent. Moreover, in the elections too many opposition candidates withdrew or were dis qualified for the voting to carry much conviction. One thing though is clear: the people of Kashmir do not mind passionately to which country they belong, provided they are left to run themselves. They would prefer independence but do not feel very strongly about it. Since Kashmir's accession to India there have been three riots, twice when Sheikh Abdullah was arrested, and far more serious, when thieves stole a treasured relic – a hair of the Prophet. Kashmiris have never rioted for or against accession to India or to Pakistan; they agree with Sheikh Abdullah who once said that instead of asking the Kashmiris to decide, India and Pakistan ought to go and fight it out, in the Punjab.

Another consequence of Partition was the dispute over the canal waters of the Punjab which nearly drove India and Pakistan to war. As a result of Partition the headworks are in India and most of the canals in Pakistan. Moreover, the Indian Punjab was not irrigated and Pakistan realized that India would soon want to divert the water for her own use. The ensuing quarrel was bitter. Fortunately it was taken under the wing of the World Bank which is helping India to finance part of the cost on Pakistan to replace from its own sources the water which comes from India.

Beside the problems arising from Partition India had to tackle all at once the problem of absorbing the princely states, of reconciling the Services to Congress rule, and of working out a linguistic formula which would consolidate the nation. The first two problems were brilliantly solved by Sardar Patel; the third was slowly muddled through by Pandit Nehru; in the end, all three have been solved.

After 15 August 1947 the princes could not continue as sovereigns if India was to be one instead of 563 nations. The princely states had been sovereign; they had their own laws, their own administration, their own army; only in Defence, Communications and Foreign Affairs had they been under the Viceroy by virtue of a series of Treaties.

There were 562 princely states, ranging from the size of a bowling green to 82,000 square miles. One third of India's territory and population was under princely rule; and, under the law, there was nothing the government of India could do to bring the princes under its wing since all of them were legally sovereign. With the help of Lord Mountbatten and V.P. Menon, a senior civil servant, Sardar Patel tackled the issue with great ingenuity. First the princes were persuaded to accede to the Indian Union, then to give up their special position. Sardar Patel and V.P. Menon managed to convince their

Highnesses that they had little choice. They could not stand out on their own because the people in their states would not support them either in absolutism or in struggle against India. Therefore, Sardar Patel and V. P. Menon argued, the princes should be content with safe incomes and a recognized position in exchange for accession to India. The princes who had been reared by the British in gilded kindergartens felt lost in the world of 1947 where what mattered was political support, instead of the statutory number of gun-salutes. When they saw, therefore, a lifebelt of tax-free privy purses which would still make them the richest men in India, they grabbed it. However, the gilt was slowly to wear off; income tax and supertax have been applied to princely investments in government securities and equities; when death duties were introduced the princes got exemption only for their privy purse – which was in any case reduced for the heir according to the terms of accession – and they have been repeatedly bullied into voluntary cuts of their privy purses. Many princes have gone into politics, some in opposition to the Congress, others on Congress tickets. So long as they are not anti-India they still enjoy the affection of their people and find it easier to get elected than professional politicians. In addition some princes have, like the Duke of Bedford in Britain, turned their palaces – those white elephants which are so costly to maintain – into de luxe hotels for tourists. Many have become investors in real estate and industry, some run cinemas or breed camels for the army. Whatever they do, they are not looked upon, nor indeed do they see themselves, as victims of revolution. They know that times have changed, indeed if one of them were to become Prime Minister of India, which is not inconceivable, there would be no restoration. The princes, like British sovereigns, have found their place in the modern world. Besides getting the 562 Indian states to join India, Sardar Patel, again with the help of V. P. Menon, started an immense programme of integration. The administration of princely India had to be brought into line with that of the ex-British India. This has been no mean task when there were as many types of administrators and laws as there were princely whims. Some states were purely feudal, others were as advanced as the best run Indian province; but even those had different administrative and tax structures which all had to be brought into one overall pattern.

At Independence the servants of the old British government, the civil servants, the policemen and the army officers found themselves in a false position. While they had been co-operating with the imperial power, the politicians who had now come into office had been in jail. Indeed, very often it was they who had put their new masters in jail, and had compiled the files on which they had been convicted. In addition the transfer of power was partly a transfer of power from them. Under the British a soldier was minister for defence, civil servants were ministers and governors; this was now all reserved for politicians. There was a much wider gap between politician and official than that of purely political views. The officials were, with exceptions, better educated than the politicians and came from a higher class than that of the average Congressman. More important still, the officials valued the gracious living intro-duced to India by their British colleagues: the clubs, the drinks, the flower-beds, the school ties, the Western suits. They shared the Britisher's belief that government knows best what is good for India. Congress in 1947, largely because of Gandhi, still made a fetish of austerity, prohibition, handspun village clothes, and held strongly to the belief that they alone knew what was good for India; moreover they looked with distaste upon the spacious bungalows of the officials – though that did not stop them commandeering them for themselves. For 30 years the Congress had been attacking not only the official's power but also his pay. The old public servants, whose terms of service had been guaranteed under the 1935 Act, were still receiving the same pay as pre-war though the cost of living had risen over three and a half times. Nevertheless Congress leaders, parti-cularly Pandit Nehru, talked of cutting their pay. Sardar Patel was quick to perceive not only that Indian officials were just as patriotic as politicians, but also that if they were not made to feel wanted they would serve without enthusiasm. Without losing a moment he announced that guarantees of the terms of service of the imperial servants would be incorporated in the Constitution and that the services had a key part to play in India's future. The fact that Sardar Patel was right has been shown by the devotion with which civil servants have worked twelve hours a day and more, and by the high standard of administration India enjoys to this day – the best between Paris and Tokyo – despite the fact that the administration is overstrained. The service has too much to do and is still suffering from wartime dilution; there is too much political interference as well as increasing corruption at the lower levels. Yet, despite all its defects, the machine is still a magnificent one; it does the old jobs of keeping law and order as well as ever and does many more things in addition; from planning to rural credit, from making antibiotics to steel.

The old Indian Civil Service has been succeeded by the Indian Administrative Service which gets less pay but nearly as much talent, though it is handicapped by lack of systematic on-the-job training and growing political pressures. The police continues as before. The armed forces on the other hand have become the beloved of the nation for their heroic defence of Kashmir and their excellent record abroad under the United Nations Flag; but above all for their readiness to help in natural calamities and for their impeccable behaviour. The armed forces have kept aloof from politics partly because that has been their tradition but also because Sardar Patel saw to it that none of the heroes of the Indian National Army who defected to Japan during the war benefited from their aberration. The public does not hold against them the *débâcle* in Assam against the Chinese in 1962 because of the widespread feeling that the armed forces had been let down by the Defence Minister Krishna Menon whose dismissal was imposed upon Nehru by public opinion.

There are 14 official languages in India[2] and over 800 dialects. In British days Hindustani, a cross between Urdu and Hindi, was used as the *lingua franca* in the armed forces. Hindustani could be written in any script and was widely understood all over India; indeed Gandhi had recommended that it should become India's official language. However, purists from the Hindi speaking parts of India – Bihar and Uttar Pradesh – objected and after prolonged discussions it was decided by one vote that Hindi would become the national language while English would be retained only for a transition period of 15 years. This decision was unwise. To begin with Hindi, which is understood only by a third of India's population, is a language arrested in its growth because it was displaced first by Urdu then by English in a way in which Bengali, Tamil, Telugu, Malayalam, Gujerati or Marathi for example were not. To bring Hindi up to date, 300,000 words are in the process of being created by the Language Commission appointed for the purpose. Since the members of the commission are stubborn and scholarly they have been coining complicated Sanskrit derivations to replace perfectly well known words. Thus 'terrain' understood to mean 'train' from Lake Mansarovar to Cape Comorin, is now the Sanskrit for 'the fire chariot which runs on metal lines' while 'radio' has become 'the celestial voice', with the result that Hindi broadcasts are unintelligible even to Hindi speakers. It is quite common for people from the UP – the homeland of Hindi – to switch on to Radio Lahore in order to follow the news.

South India, where Hindi is not known, has been protesting with great vigour against 'Hindi imperialism', and there have been so many anti-Hindi riots and demonstrations that in the end a compromise was reached. Nehru announced that English would, by constitutional amendment, become an 'associate' language which would be retained side by side with Hindi. Nobody outside the Hindi speaking area objects to English as the *lingua franca*. The disadvantages of Hindi are so obvious that they need not be listed, while the advantages of English are so obvious that all those parents who can afford to send their children to schools where English is the medium of instruction do so, because English is not only a window to the outside world but it also provides an immediate contact with the sciences and the arts independent of translations which will always be both obsolescent and restricted due to cost.

One of the effects of trying to push Hindi down people's throats has been that they have turned to their own regional languages with jingoistic fervour; as a result less English and more regional languages has been taught at school. Inter-state communication therefore and particularly movement from one university to the other, for students and staff alike, is being hampered; thus endangering a cultural unity to which the spread of English has been fundamental. Fortunately there are signs that commonsense will prevail and gradually English is resuming much of its old place in secondary education, although there is difficulty in finding enough qualified teachers.

The language issue was allowed to fester at the expense of national unity and educational efficiency for so long first because Nehru, to whom all sides looked for advice, was not able to persuade the language fanatics that his own predilection for English did not make him partial; in addition he hesitated to overrule them for the sake of Indian unity.

After Nehru the language issue took a sudden turn for the worse on 26 January 1965 as a result of the new Prime Minister's action. Mr Lal Bahadur Shastri, in every other aspect a most moderate man, is a Hindi fanatic. He is the first Central Minister to have addressed Parliament in Hindi. He was also responsible for issuing all railway booking-offices with forms and tickets in Hindi to the total disarray of clerks and customers in southern India who could not fill in the forms which consequently had to be withdrawn. He announced that the Official Languages Act would take effect from 26 January in accordance with the Constitution, and advised the south to speed up the process of learning Hindi. As a result severe rioting broke out in Madras and later in Andhra. Damage to property ran into millions of pounds, casualties into thousands, and fatalities into hundreds. Peace and Indian unity could only be salvaged by announcing that English would continue as before for an indefinite period.

Besides the issue of the national language there was in addition the issue of the regional language; an issue which Nehru's indecision and weakness allowed to get out of hand. In British days India was organized into units which were not linguistic but historical. This was both cumbersome and was bound to lead to difficulties once adult franchise brought the people into politics. Gandhi had organized the Congress on a linguistic basis because he felt that the only way to reach the masses was to appeal to them in their mother tongue. Soon after Independence, the various linguistic Congress groups began to agitate for a linguistic redistribution of the states boundaries. Some states like Bombay or Hyderabad were trilingual, while others, like the United Provinces or Bengal were unilingual. Nehru, who feared the fissiparous effect of a linguistic reorganization of the country, did not want linguistic states. However, when the people's demand became violent, deprived by Sardar Patel's death of the courage of his convictions, Nehru gave way in one case, and Madras was divided on linguistic lines into the states of Madras and Andhra. The lesson was not lost on the public. If violence was the means to get their way, they would resort to violence. After a spate of rioting Nehru reluctantly agreed to appoint a Commission to redraw the administrative map of India on linguistic lines. Eventually after some muddling by Nehru and serious riots in Bombay, the map was redrawn on linguistic lines. The demand for linguistic states had been so strong because under the Constitution a great amount of the day to day administration which affects people's lives is done by the state; and people like to be run in their own language by men of their own group.

The extent to which the administration has so far been successful in making India develop is indeed a tribute to its skill for one must not forget that India is a Federal state. Federation, combined to the degree of local autonomy which the Constitution devolves upon the states must produce a weak Centre and make central planning very difficult. Indeed the main links between the Centre and the units are the All-India Services, the defence forces, financial control and as a last resort the provision under the Constitution by which, in the public interest, the Prime Minister can, on the advice of the President, supersede a local government and promulgate President's Rule for a maximum period of one year.

To illustrate the difficulties arising from this weak Federalism, let us take the saga of the Grow More Food Campaign. Way back in 1951 Nehru announced that India would be self-sufficient in food grains by the end of the First Five-Year Plan. India is still today far from being self-sufficient although food production has undoubtedly been going up but not fast enough.[3] This mitigated failure can be attributed to the fact that food and agriculture is a state and not a central subject.

5   The Constitution

WE THE PEOPLE OF INDIA, having solemnly resolved to constitute India into a SOVEREIGN, DEMOCRATIC REPUBLIC and to secure to all its citizens:
JUSTICE, social economic and political;
LIBERTY of thought, expression, belief, faith and worship;
EQUALITY of status and of opportunity;
and to promote against them all
FRATERNITY assuring the dignity of the individual and the unity of the Nation;
IN OUR CONSTITUENT ASSEMBLY...DO HEREBY ADOPT, ENACT AND GIVE TO OURSELVES THIS CONSTITUTION. Thus reads the Preamble of the Indian Constitution of 1950 which embodies all the aspirations of the Congress Party and lays down that India should (1) be a Parliamentary Democracy; (2) be a Federal state; (3) be a Republic; (4) have a written Constitution; (5) be a member of the Commonwealth; (6) be a Secular state; (7) be a Welfare state.

India became a Federal Republic on 26 January 1950 when the Constitution came into effect; until that moment India had been run by an interim arrangement – with a Governor-General instead of a Viceroy – under the Government of India Act of 1935 with a few modifications to suit the changed relationship with Britain. The Indian Constitution is in effect based upon the Government of India Act which has been adapted to suit the requirements of universal adult franchise and equality. This development of the

Constitution from the Government of India Act explains why India's Federalism gives so much power to the Centre. It is a Federation imposed from above, not, as in the case of the United States of America from below.[4] The Government of India Act had been devised by the British to provide a tight central control over the federal units. The Constitution of 1950 embodies most of this control. Article 3 authorizes the Central Parliament by a simple majority to form new states and to alter state boundaries without the consent of the states concerned. It was under Article 3 that the linguistic redistribution of India was carried out. Article 249 gives Parliament powers to legislate on matters included in the State List if it has a two-thirds majority. Articles 352 to 360 contain the emergency provisions by which the President is empowered to suspend the Constitution and take over the administration of a state or states of the Indian Union if he is satisfied that there is a threat to security, to the Constitution, or if there is a financial emergency. The powers of the Centre and the States are enumerated in three lists: a Union List, a State List and a Concurrent List.

The Executive Branch of the Indian government is headed by the President – who, as President, is above party. He is chosen by an electoral college of both Houses of Parliament and the state legislatures for a term of five years. He can be re-elected but can only be removed by impeachment. The President's relation with the Prime Minister and the cabinet is similar to that of the British Sovereign with the addition of the special powers under articles 352 to 360 which give him very extensive powers in case of emergency but these can only be exercised on the advice of the cabinet. However, the President must issue a Proclamation before he can act; there is a normal time limit of six months after the Proclamation for which his special powers remain valid, and the state of emergency cannot be extended for more than three years. Between 1950 and 1960 the President used his emergency powers five times to restore law and order in the states.[5] In all these cases the President acted with due regard to democratic interests.

The Vice-President is elected by both Houses of Parliament for a period of five years and is *ex-officio* Chairman of the Upper House.

The Prime Minister and the cabinet are theoretically bound to each other by collective responsibility to Parliament in the British way, though Nehru as Prime Minister exercised an ascendancy over his colleagues even stronger than that of British prime ministers.

The Central Parliament consists of 500 members elected for a period of five years on universal adult franchise from constituencies of not more than half a million votes each. The Upper House has a limited membership of 250 – 12 of whom are nominated by the President to represent the arts and the professions. The remaining 238 are elected by the State Legislatures. Members of the Upper House are not removable, they serve for six years but one third of them retire every two years – they can of course be re-elected. The Upper House is the Indian equivalent of the House of Lords.

The Central Parliament has jurisdiction over defence, foreign affairs, communications, currency and banking, inter-state trade, mineral resources and food. The State List includes law and order, the police, local government, public health, education, agriculture and irrigation. The Concurrent List includes criminal law, personal law, property law, civil law, trade unions, labour disputes, and trade and commerce.

The Indian Constitution is the longest in the world: it has 250 pages, 395 articles and innumerable provisions. This is deliberate. When the Constitution was adopted a senior Congressman told Parliament:

> There are two things that the British have left behind for us; one is the efficiency of the Civil Service and the other is the Rule of Law. And I think both . . . have been incorporated in this Constitution, because without an efficient Civil Service it will be impossible for the government to be carried on and for the continuity of policy to be kept. . . . Unless there is continuity there is bound to be chaos. . . . The Rule of Law . . . if there is anything I would like to cling to in the future of this country it is this Rule of Law. . . . I think we have provided in the Constitution, in the powers vested both in the Supreme Court and the High Courts . . . for any citizen to have his right established as against the government of the day.

By choice as well as by nature, the Indian leaders were careful to limit their own powers, by insisting that everything has to be done under the law. India is a Rechtsstaat. To be arbitrary might often enable the government to move more quickly, but it has specifically bound itself not to be arbitrary. The Constitution gives the individual citizen nearly as many fundamental rights as does that of the United States of America; and the government has, so far, respected the Constitution scrupulously. The checks which the government has imposed upon itself are very real. The Judiciary is independent of the executive; there is a Supreme Court at the head of the judicial hierarchy with High Courts in each of the states. The courts have time and again shown their independence; for example when they held that the government should not prevent children whose mother tongue is English from going to schools where English is the medium of instruction. They have held that the government cannot take over the management of a badly run concern without paying compensation for the management's loss of the right to manage; that the government cannot legally create a road transport monopoly for itself; that a state government cannot prohibit the use of medicinal wine (under the provisions of Pro-hibition Laws); that compensation for property taken over must be at market value and so on. Some of these decisions, especially about compensation, have been met by changes in the Constitution or the law; but the alterations themselves have been made in proper form, with the required constitutional majorities. There has never been a case where the executive has defied the courts, or has tried to impose its will regardless of the law.

The Indian government is elected and never forgets it. Just as it does not force its views on the electorate it responds to the electorate's views once they have crystallized into votes. Thus there is in India a real working democracy, which expresses itself through the work-ings of politics.

The features of Indian political life which make it so different from the other newly independent states go deep into India's past; to the eighteenth-century High Courts in the Presidency Towns; to Macaulay's Penal Code and Minute on Education; to the

Government of India Acts of 1919 and 1935 with their widening electorates and increasingly responsible government. Above all they go back to Mahatma Gandhi's endless willingness to negotiate and wait until he had convinced his opponent. It was Gandhi who developed the technique of progressive change, perhaps on the British model, in which one keeps the best of the old and takes the best of the new. This technique is also profoundly Hindu. Hindus dislike drastic measures, they do not approve of enforcing on others decisions taken by a body of self-appointed men who claim to know what is best. India has a long past of local self-government, for until the British came she had never had a really effective central government, or indeed a really centralized state. Hindu history is a history of tolerance, of persuasion. Its Calvin was the Lord Buddha. It is typical that the Indian National Day is not 15 August, the day the British left India, but 26 January, the day India became a Republic.

Key to the spirit in which the Constitution was framed is the determination to bring about social equality, and reassure the minorities. This spirit is embodied in the Fundamental Rights of the Constitution which lay down that: 'The state shall not discriminate against any citizen on grounds only of religion, race, caste, sex, place of birth. . . . No citizen shall, on grounds only of religion, race, caste, sex, place of birth . . . be subject to any disability, liability, restriction or condition with regard to access to shops, public restaurants, hotels and places of public entertainment or the use of wells, tanks, bathing ghats, roads and places of public resort maintained wholly or partly out of state funds or dedicated to the use of the general public.' This is much further than the British dared to go. It hits at the root of untouchability. Indeed, the Constitution makes this quite clear, for it goes on to lay down that: 'Untouchability is abolished and its practice in any form is forbidden. The enforcement of any disability arising out of untouchability shall be an offence punishable in accordance with law.' The onus of proof that there has been no breach of the law is put upon the accused, not as in the case of Negroes in America, on the complainant.

Indians are guaranteed under their Constitution the traditional rights of free men everywhere: freedom of speech and expression; of

peaceful assembly, associations, movement and residence; of property, profession, business or occupation; and of worship. The Fundamental Rights in all take up 12 pages of the Constitution.

In addition to the Fundamental Rights, to redeem Gandhi's pledge that the Harijans – the Children of God – as he called the Untouchables, would get every opportunity of becoming full citizens, the state provides for them, as well as reserved electoral seats in Parliament and the state legislatures, the reservation of government jobs, places in colleges and hostels and generous grants of all kinds. The amounts spent by the Central government on Untouchable uplift has gone up from just over £5 million in the First Five-Year Plan to £18 million in the Second Five-Year Plan and £30 million in the Third Five-Year Plan in addition to the £23 million which are earmarked for their benefit by the states. As a result of this financial effort the number of Untouchables at secondary schools has gone up from 600,000 in 1956–7 to 900,000 in 1961 and the number of Untouchables who have gone on to study beyond matriculation has risen from 1,100 to 40,000 in the same period.

While Parliamentary democracy has been under attack in so many newly independent states, in India it still flourishes. There have been three general elections, there has been no attempt to suppress the opposition, and voting has increased each time! As Nehru himself once told Parliament:

We chose this system of parliamentary democracy deliberately; we chose it not only because to some extent we had always thought on those lines previously, but because we thought it was in keeping with our own old traditions . . . adjusted to the new conditions and new surroundings. We chose it – let us give credit where credit is due – because we approved of its functioning in other countries, more especially in the United Kingdom.

34 The first Indian social reformer was Ram Mohan Roy (1774–1833), who founded the Brahmo Samaj, a Hindu casteless sect. A nineteenth-century engraving.

35 Under paramountcy in the nineteenth century the princes were protected by the British in exchange for loyalty. An early photograph of a prince, his family and British civilians.

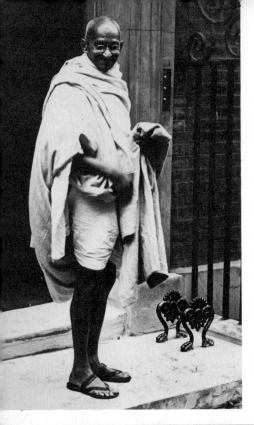

36 India's greatest leader, Mohandas Karam-chand Gandhi, strongly opposed British rule and paved the way for India's independence. A photograph taken in 1931 outside No. 10 Downing Street.

37 For his policy of non-co-operation Gandhi was committed to prison on many occasions. He was released from Yeravda gaol in 1933 as seen here.

38 (*above right*) He identified himself with the mass of the Indian people and insisted that all his followers spent some time every day in hand-spinning.

39 (*centre right*) One of his prime concerns was Hindu-Muslim unity. On the Noahkali tour in 1946 he talked to Muslim peasants.

40 (*below right*) At Delhi in 1947 he patiently listened to grievances voiced by Muslims.

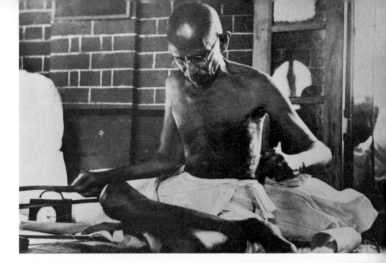

41 The Simon Commission sent by Britain in 1928 was boycotted because it did not include an Indian member.

42 In 1942 Sir Stafford Cripps attempted to placate Gandhi but failed. This precipitated the 'Quit India' movement.

43 British hesitation over the Bengal famine in 1943 resulted in further distrust among India's people. The Viceroy, Lord Wavell, visiting a food kitchen.

44 In 1947 the British Empire of India ended; three years later Prime Minister Nehru signed the Constitution of an independent republic.

45 Mahomed Ali Jinnah (1876–1948) was the leader of Hindu-Muslim separatism from 1930. He founded the Muslim state of Pakistan in 1940.

46 But this partitioning of India eventually created new problems. At the Khyber Pass, Pakistan's Afghan frontier.

47 Hindu refugees who pour into India from Pakistan have to be rehabilitated. This is at Calcutta.

48 The struggle between India and Pakistan over the ownership of Kashmir is an unsettled problem. This typical Kashmiri scene is at Srinagar.

49 Lord Louis Mountbatten was sent by the British government in 1947 to prepare the blueprint for the transfer of power.

50 After Independence India was led by two men: Pandit Jawaharlal Nehru and Sardar Patel.

51 Republic Day is an annual celebration at New Delhi.

6 Impact

ONE OF THE DIRECTIVE PRINCIPLES of the Constitution lays down that there will be free compulsory education for all children up to the age of 14; it is hoped that by 1966 over half the children between the ages of 6 and 11 will be at school. The number of schools in the villages doubled in the first 14 years after Independence, and by 1966 there will be 34 million children at school. Three-quarters of the people are still illiterate but male literacy had gone up to 34 per cent by 1961. The pattern of literacy is, however, far from uniform; thus in Kerala the rate of literacy is very high, 60 per cent, while it is very low in Bihar or Uttar Pradesh. Moreover there are three times as many men who can read as women and there are many cases of people recorded as literate lapsing into illiteracy again due to lack of practice.

Education is not a federal subject; each state does what it likes. The result is that there has not been enough adaptation of the curriculum to changed circumstances. One can still find children learning to convert shillings into pence although British currency never bore any relation to Indian currency which is now based upon the decimal system.[6] Too many primers are still encumbered with sentences like 'the cow is your mother and your father'. The medium of instruction in all primary schools is the vernacular.

Running efficient primary schools in India is immensely difficult. There are not enough good textbooks and not enough trained teachers, particularly not enough women teachers, which means that many parents will not send their daughters to school.

These difficulties are inherent in the Indian situation with more than 840,000 rural communities, of which over 80 per cent are hamlets inhabited by less than five hundred people. One third of India's population live in such small hamlets while another 12 per cent live in villages with populations of between 500 and 1,000. When half the population of India – 238,000,000 people – live in villages of under 1,000, to provide enough schools becomes very difficult because of the number of teachers required.[7] Moreover, teachers, particularly if they are women, do not like living in villages unless their husbands have a place in the life of the village. It is also not possible to provide a teacher for each village; this means that pupils may have to walk up to five miles to go to school; and this in turn means that many girls do not go even if they are not wanted to mind babies or goats. With so few teachers it is not possible to have more than one teacher per school. This means that all the pupils sit together, some still barely able to count their fingers and decipher the alphabet while others are already doing multiplication and taking dictation. They seldom get much beyond the latter stage at primary school. Primary education is already compulsory in a few states and there are over 35 million children in primary schools or 60 per cent of that age group.

Secondary education is usually conducted in the vernacular, with English taught as a second language and Hindi as a third language. There are not enough Hindi teachers and there have been so many changes in the teaching of English, which used in British days to be the medium of secondary instruction, that there is a great shortage of English teachers. The result is that the standard of English has dropped very sharply although the number of English speakers has gone up. This is why parents who can afford to send their children to those private schools which still use English as the medium of instruction do so, even when it means a considerable financial sacrifice. There are in addition a few residential public schools to which the *élite* send their children by putting their name down at birth as is the practice in Britain.

There has been a real explosion in post-primary education since Independence as the figures show. In 1947 there were three million students in secondary schools all over the country, and in 1960 there were 18 million. Unless they get grants because they are Untouchable or Backward, the students have to pay a fee, and since there are hardly any secondary schools in the villages, they also have to pay for hostel accommodation and food. Only just over one student in ten has a grant. Secondary schools are multiplying as fast as teachers and buildings can be provided. The number of teachers must go up by 50,000 a year to keep pace with the programme. There are now (1965) well over 67,000 secondary schools, and in addition there are some 4,300 multi-purpose high schools which give training in agriculture and crafts as well as the arts. There are also well over 200 free industrial training institutes with some 100,000 places.[8]

University education has not quite kept pace with the spread of secondary education. There are 54 universities in India; 17 of them are making an attempt to get away from English as the medium of instruction, and offer some courses in Hindi or the regional language. One of the major problems all universities have to face is that most of the students know so little English that they find it difficult to follow lectures, particularly when the classrooms are overcrowded and there are not enough lecturers or textbooks. In 1857 there were three universities in India; in 1947 their number had gone up considerably and there were already 200,000 students enlisted at college or university. By 1962, barely 15 years later, there were over a million students enrolled at university. This multiplication has been achieved at some expense of quality and most of the universities have such a low standard both of teaching and admission that their degrees are worth little, though this is of course not true of some of the older and more established institutions where dilution is no greater than at a British 'Redbrick'. That there is much room for improvement is shown by the fact that 50 per cent of those who are admitted fail their intermediate examination and of the 50 per cent who pass, 40 per cent fail their finals.

In addition to the expansion of the universities, 25 Central Government Research Institutes have been set up since 1947. These institutes compete with the universities for post graduates, money and equipment so that their very existence makes it difficult for the universities to develop their science departments beyond the elementary teaching stage.

Communications

Means of communication, so important in the formulation of political attitudes, are still fairly primitive in India. Less than 22,000 villages and towns have electricity. There is no *proper* television as yet – radio sets are mostly battery run and the radio is controlled by the Ministry of Information.

There are 36 transmitting stations; radio sets are fairly frequent in the cities but in the villages they are still very much the exception. There are over four million radio sets in India, of which 600,000 are in villages (400,000 of these are privately owned; the rest are owned by the village). The programmes are broadcast in the regional languages and in Hindi; there are also English news bulletins. Radio stations concentrate on agricultural news, including price of crops and weather forecasts, on religious drama and classical music, as well as on lengthy government handouts. Political broadcasts are not allowed.

Only one village in ten has a post-office of sorts, this also limits the extent to which news can come in. After the radio there is the newspaper. In 1960 there were 342 daily newspapers with a combined circulation of over four million. Of these 43 were English language papers, and between them they covered nearly 23 per cent of the circulation. The rest of the papers were printed in regional languages. In India circulation is not an indication of readership or influence since newspapers are handed on from reader to reader perhaps as many as four times. Often in the village the illiterates sit around to listen as the paper is read out by the school teacher or the matriculate home for a visit from the town.

Public opinion in India is fairly homogeneous – except when it comes to local issues. The most important person in creating public opinion is the matriculate. The matriculate usually lives in the city where he imbibes the views of those better educated than himself, through the newspaper or by listening to political rallies, and thrashes things out with his friends at the coffee house and his neighbours at home and at work. It is the matriculate who brings back to his village the wisdom of the town every time there is a wedding, a death, or some family gathering. Because he is educated and has a smattering of English, he is listened to with the result that what he says often carries a disproportionate weight. Over the 15 years the author has lived in India, it has been possible to trace the spread of public opinion from the *élite*, through the clerk, to the peasant, within a relatively short time. Thus by the end of 1958 there were a few leaders in industry and government who criticized Nehru; by the beginning of 1960 these same criticisms were widely expressed even in the remoter villages. In 1964, when Nehru died, Lal Bahadur Shastri was elected Prime Minister by the Congress High Command. The appointment was unanimous and reflected public opinion. A Gallup poll taken at the beginning of that year showed Lal Bahadur Shastri to be the favourite. Over 40 per cent of those asked had chosen him to succeed Nehru; this gave him more than an 80 per cent margin over the next candidate. Lal Bahadur Shastri is a modest, honest, hard working man – a Kayastha by caste he comes from the middle class, received a classical Sanskrit education and went abroad for the first time as Prime Minister.

Eminently reasonable and unassuming, Lal Bahadur Shastri will continue the essentials of Nehru's policies while dropping those that have failed. He has already settled the old quarrel with Ceylon and brought a certain sense of realism into planning, and his refusal to match China's first nuclear explosions has been courageous, but this may in fact not continue. However, there is a growing impatience amongst Indians because of his tendency to try to govern by consent instead of bullying the chief ministers to nominal assent. Nehru had created the erroneous impression that his word was law; in fact his word used to remain unchallenged but unimplemented. Lal Bahadur Shastri by contrast believes in making announcements only after he is satisfied that action will follow. There is nevertheless substance in the feeling that he should be less permissive especially in the matter of enforcing an All-India food policy.

Elections
In 1947 the great majority of those who were not Muslim were Congress. The Congress Party had the aura of the national move-ment which had taken India into freedom, and there was also

Gandhi's magnetism. Indeed, the Congress, under the British, had been a national movement, not a political party. Except for the communists and the extreme right-wing Hindu-Mahasabha, everybody who was in the slightest bit politically or nationally minded, was Congress. Already in 1939 the Congress had three million members, and covered the whole spectrum from those who, like Gandhi, believed in village self-sufficiency and non-violence, to those who believed in violence, socialism and industrialization.

The first general election on universal adult franchise was held in 1951-2, the second in 1957, the third in 1962. The stability of Indian politics emerges clearly if one looks at what happened in these elections.

In the first place the percentage of voting remained almost the same with about 54 per cent of the electorate casting their vote. Next, Congress support remained remarkably static at around 45 per cent of the vote. Equally in terms of seats, as distinct from votes, there was remarkably little change. The Congress has been able to hold three-quarters of the Parliamentary seats and two-thirds of the State Assembly seats. The other parties, the socialists, the communists, the communalist parties have more or less maintained their position; any changes that have taken place have occurred either from division within these parties themselves or from taking votes away from independent candidates. The last election was marked by the weakening of the Socialist Party and the emergence of the new right-wing Swatantra Party. The communists, despite growing anxiety about India's dispute with China (the elections preceded the Chinese invasion of Assam), managed to retain their position.

However, such electoral conservatism does not mean that the electorate is apathetic or that the elections are rigged. On the contrary, elections have become as much part of Indian life as football pools have of British life. Indians love voting, everybody turns up; the women dressed in fineries as for a social event. Elections are run by the Election Commission which is totally independent of the government and has a great reputation for efficiency and impartiality. Moreover, disgruntled candidates can complain to the Election Tribunal which is above suspicion; the fact that so few of them do

is proof that the elections are both free and fair, and that the opposition is not throttled. Indeed in 1957 the electorate threw out no less
than 28 ministers, including two chief ministers, and defeated the
Congress government of Kerala.

Due to the size of the operation, the elections are the most spectacular demonstration that India is a functioning democracy based on
the rule of law and the parliamentary system with freedom to dis-
agree and oppose.

In 1962 there were 210 million voters on the electoral rolls; and no
less than 1,680,000 people were employed to look after the 240,000
polling stations and count the votes. Polling stations have, by
statute, to be within three miles of the voters' homes and, wherever
required, special voting facilities have to be provided for women as
many of them are still in semi-seclusion. With so many illiterate
voters the process of voting is somewhat more complicated than it is
in the West. Once the voter has been identified by his number
against the electoral roll he is given a ballot paper with the symbols
of the different parties or candidates on it and told to mark the symbol
of his choice in the privacy of the electoral booth before he folds his
ballot paper and places it in the ballot box in front of the returning
officer who marks his wrist with indelible ink so that he cannot
vote twice.

In 1962 16 parties were given official recognition by the Election
Commission and in addition the elections were contested by a large
number of independents. In all, independent candidates polled over
12 per cent of the vote, more than anybody except the Congress
Party. Independent candidates are often disgruntled Congressmen
who have been refused a Congress ticket, or individuals who count
on the backing of a particular caste, or ex-princes who have refused
to join a party and are popular in their own area.

Let us now consider the political parties in more detail.

THE CONGRESS PARTY
The Congress Party has been in office since 1947. It has never secured
over 48 per cent of the total votes but no other party has secured over
11 per cent. In the Central Parliament there are 361 (in 1962) out of

494 elected members and Congress has always had more than 73 per cent of the seats because of the fragmentation of the opposition.

The Congress Party stands for socialism, planning, welfare and neutralism in foreign policy. Its programme is reflected in the way India has been going since Independence. This is because the Congress Party has not yet recovered from the fact that it began not as a political party but as a national movement. As a result its membership covers a very much wider spectrum than that of British political parties, though not very different from American political parties which can accommodate Senators Goldwater and Fulbright under one label. Indian Congressmen can, like Mr Desai or Mr Patil, believe in free enterprise and be pro-Western or like Mr Krishna Menon be pro-communist and want everything nationalized.

THE COMMUNIST PARTY

In 1957 the communists polled nearly 9 per cent of the vote; in 1962 they got just under 10 per cent. They now have 29 seats in Parliament.

The membership of the Communist Party has never been large; it was estimated at some 178,000 in 1962, the Chinese attack on India having lost them 40,000 members. Party membership represents less than 2 per cent of the votes the communists get at election time because most of the communist votes are votes of protest against specific Congress policies or failures of implementation, not votes for Marxism.

The communists have only once won an election, which was in 1957 in the state of Kerala. They captured 65 seats – an absolute majority of one – and were able to form the government. After 28 months of misgovernment and a widespread popular agitation for their removal they were dismissed by Presidential Proclamation, and a coalition of the Congress, the socialists and the Muslim League won the election inflicting a landslide defeat on the communists who only got 29 seats. The percentage though of the communist vote went up by 4 per cent to 43 per cent and it did look as if the communists might win again in Kerala, not because of their own virtue but because of the vices of the local Congress Party.

Traditionally the communists are strong in two states besides Kerala: Andhra where they have the support of the Kammas,[9] and in West Bengal where they have the support of the refugees from East Pakistan and of many of the urban lower middle class. This explains their strength in the city of Calcutta.[10]

The history of the Indian Communist Party is an object lesson in what happens when directives come from outside. The party was founded in 1924 – and its top leadership has had a high level of continuity. One of the founders, Mr S.A. Dange, is still the leader and takes his orders from Moscow. During the 1930s the communists worked from within the Congress Party; by 1939 there were 20 of them on the All-India Congress Committee – the Congress Party Convention. But in 1941 they had to leave the Congress because the Congress was against the war on the ground that it was imperialist, while for the communists, Germany's attack on Russia transformed it into a people's war. From 1941 to the end of the war the Communist Party co-operated with the British; this did it a great deal of harm in Indian eyes. In 1948 an International Communist Conference was held in Calcutta; Moscow issued a secret directive urging active subversion and violence. As a result Indian communists concentrated on burning trams in Calcutta and carrying out a successful guerrilla war against landlords and the government in the Telengana area of Hyderabad. After three years of fighting the Indian army managed to restore law and order in Telengana with the help of the extraordinary personal appeal of India's walking saint, Vinoba Bhave, Gandhi's spiritual heir. Vinoba Bhave appealed to the landed to give land to the landless; and he managed to create such a response for his 'Bhoodan' – land-gift – that the bitterness on which the communists had thrived in Telengana vanished. Moreover, in 1951 the communists, whose party had been banned, decided that they had better eschew violence and become law-abiding in order to be able to contest the elections.

For a time they did fairly well in opposition, exploiting local grievances. The next blow to the Indian Communist Party came when China first invaded part of Ladakh in 1957 and then far more seriously drove the Indian army back into Assam in 1962. Most damaging of all has been the Sino-Soviet rift which has divided the Indian communists between the Moscow group, still led by Mr Dange who favours the parliamentary process, and the Peking group strong above all in Bengal, which favours the revolutionary process.

Communism has little attraction for the Indian people who are profoundly religious and permissive. The social structure does not lend itself to a Marxist class war.

The Untouchables are not organized and they are everywhere in a minority. Apart from this the Congress Party is doing so much for them that the communists could hardly do more.

The industrial proletariat, which is only a few million strong, has few grievances. Of all the sections of the Indian population it has been doing best; its pay is more directly related to the cost of living than that of anybody else; it is heavily protected by legislation; indeed Indian labour laws are so biased in favour of the workers that they create a disincentive to industrial expansion.

The *élite*, the educated middle class which provided so much of the leadership in Russia and China, has little cause for grievance for it has come into power with the advent of Independence by providing the managerial and administrative talent with which to run the country. The 'ci-devants', the ones who have been dispossessed, the big landlords, the princes, the moneylenders are not likely to start Marxist revolutions.

Finally, organized violence – as distinct from the violent explosion of the normally repressed and peaceful – has no appeal for a people who are both profoundly religious and loath to the taking of even animal life. Therefore, unless India is overrun by China, which the West is not likely to allow, or there is a communist *coup d'état* with armed-force support which is equally unlikely, there are few chances indeed that India will go communist. The armed forces are much more likely to back the administration if it were to try to take over in the event of political chaos than the politicians, for the Indian armed forces are not politically minded. The British tradition that the Services are outside politics was reinforced by Sardar Patel's treatment of the rebels of the Indian National Army, none of whom were reinstated at Independence. Even Mr Krishna Menon's most arduous efforts and intrigues when he was Defence Minister failed to break the tradition.

THE SOCIALIST PARTY

Sandwiched between the Congress Party with its 'socialistic pattern' and the Communist Party, the Indian Socialist Party has little scope. Until the 1962 elections it attained a larger percentage of the vote than the Communist Party, but due to organizational and financial weakness it got fewer seats. In addition the socialists are continually splintering into rival groups or losing their best leaders to the Congress Party[11] or to the Gandhian ideal.[12] In 1957 the socialists got over 10 per cent of the vote; in 1962 they got just under 7 per cent, 179 members in the State Assemblies and 12 members in Parliament.

However, the future of the Socialist Party is perhaps brighter than that of the Communist Party. In due course, the Congress Party may split into right wing and left wing; up to now it has been kept together by Nehru's charisma and by its election machinery. Now that Nehru is dead it is possible that there will be in due course a realignment of forces within the party and there may be advantages in dividing the machinery. If this were to happen the crypto communists will be thrown out, right-wing and orthodox Congressmen may attract to their fold the right-wing parties, leaving Congress left wingers to coalesce with the socialists. It is probable that both wings of the Congress would want to keep the magic name as far as possible so that one may look to the day when India has a two-party system with the choice between the 'Socialist Congress' and the 'People's Congress'.

THE SWATANTRA PARTY

The Swatantra Party was created in 1959 by Mr C. Rajagopalachari, one of Gandhi's oldest and most experienced colleagues, to curb Nehru's leftishness. Mr Rajagopalachari, who was India's first

Indian Governor-General, had been Home Minister and Finance Minister in the Government of India and twice Chief Minister of Madras. He was stirred into action at the age of 80 by Nehru's announcement that he would introduce compulsory joint co-operative farming – an announcement Nehru had to modify immediately by saying that joint co-operative farming would be voluntary.

Swatantra means freedom; the new party stands for free enterprise, economic *laissez-faire*, trusteeship – instead of welfare – a more Western orientated foreign policy and better relations with Pakistan. In 1962 the Swatantra Party got 6·8 per cent of the vote, and became the official opposition party in Bihar, Gujerat and Rajasthan while in Orissa it negotiated a post-election merger with a locally strong party, the Ganatantra Parishad. The Swatantra Party's election record after barely three years is indeed impressive: 170 Assembly Members against the communists' 197; but only 18 Members of Parliament against the communists 29. The future of the Swatantra Party is closely linked to what happens in the Congress Party. If that party splits, many on its right wing may coalesce with the Swatantra.

THE JAN SANGH
This party is not only right-wing but also orthodox and communal, in contrast to the Swatantra Party which is right-wing but modern. The Jan Sangh Party never gets more than 6 per cent of the vote; it has secured 14 parliamentary seats (an increase of ten seats), and is the major opposition in Uttar Pradesh and Madhya Pradesh which are amongst India's most backward states. The Jan Sangh Party has some following in the cities, but so long as 85 per cent of India's population lives in the villages and constituencies are determined by the number of voters, its hopes of getting into power are utopian.[13]

MINOR PARTIES
In addition to the major parties there are some parties with a local following sufficiently strong for the Congress Party to be worried, at the state level. In the Punjab there is the Akali Dal – the Sikh

opposition party; in Madras there is the DMK which won a quarter of the seats in the local assembly on a separatist platform based on the slogans of Hindi imperialism and northern domination of south India. The DMK has a considerable nuisance value which is most useful to southern India as a whole when it comes to standing up against the distortion of Indian politics; a distortion due to the fact that Delhi, the Federal capital, is located in the north. One good example of this nuisance value was the active participation of the DMK in the 1965 anti-Hindi riots. Moreover, it is useful, when it comes to the allocation of funds, for politicians from the south to overplay dangers that the DMK might succeed in splitting India.[14]

The most complex political situation in India is to be found in the state of Kerala. It is no accident that Kerala has been India's problem state and may remain so for a long time to come. Located along the southern tip of India it has the highest literacy rate – about 60 per cent. It also has the largest number of educated unemployed, the highest density of population, the most complex social structure, and the worst political record. Caste plays a key role in Kerala because it divides society into almost irreconcilable factions. A quarter of the population belong to the toddy tapping caste, until recently Untouchable, and now progressing economically. Traditionally this caste supports the communists. Next comes the Christians and the Muslims, equal in strength with a third of the population between them. The Muslims vote Muslim League (Kerala is the only place in India which still has Muslim League candidates), the Christians tend to vote Congress. Then come the Nairs, a caste which observes the matriarchal system and supports the Congress, the communists and the socialists with more or less equal gusto. As can be seen from this complicated background, to get elected a party has to have the support of more than one group. To make things more complicated still, the political parties in Kerala are all discredited.

By 1957 the Congress had gone through five Chief Ministers, three elections and a spell of President's Rule; an insult to a highly educated electorate. The socialists had been in office once when their

19 representatives held the balance in a Congress coalition which had, as could be expected, proved ineffective. Because of his under, standable allergy to the Muslim League (although Kerala's Muslim League was not in favour of partition which had no meaning in the Kerala context, but merely asked for a larger share of power for Muslims), Nehru refused to enter into an electoral alliance with them in 1957. As a result the communists won the election of 1957, though only by a majority of one, and formed the government. They ruled Kerala for 28 months during which time they alienated every, body but their own supporters (those of the Nairs who were com, munist, the toddy tappers and some Untouchables) by the way they interfered with the running of the schools and the administration and the police, in an effort to provide jobs for toddy tappers and comrades. By the middle of 1959 Christians, Muslims and non, communist Nairs who had come to the conclusion that they were being treated as second-class citizens launched a civil disobedience movement which took such proportions that President's Rule had to be promulgated to avoid civil war. By 1960, when elections were held in Kerala, the communists, faced with a people's coalition, only managed to hold 29 seats although their percentage of the total votes actually went up. The polling had been unprecedented: 84 per cent of the electorate voted. In the new coalition government the Con, gress Party, which had an absolute majority, soon refused to honour its commitments to share power with the socialists and the Muslim League and by 1964 President's Rule had to be promulgated once more. In 1965 the parties were hopelessly split and the electorate thoroughly disheartened, with 14 contending parties who were largely made up from varying rebel Congress and communist factions. Little wonder that only 60 per cent of the electorate bothered to vote. The final results[15] mean that once again Kerala has to be submitted to President's Rule.

7   The Minorities

INDIA IS A SECULAR STATE; the Constitution lays down that there shall be no discrimination of any sort on the basis of race, colour, caste or creed.

There are many minority groups in India and so long as they do not interfere with the beliefs of the Hindu majority, they are given an honoured place in the society and, other things being equal, get, if anything, more than their numerical share of government and political jobs.

THE MUSLIMS

The Muslims are the biggest minority group in India, they number 50 million, which makes India the third largest Muslim country in the world after Indonesia and Pakistan. These Muslims are Indian by race – most of their ancestors were converts from Hinduism – but they are different from the Hindus not only in their religion but also in outlook and above all in their attitude to women.

The Indian Muslims have undoubtedly lost a great deal from the creation of a Pakistan which had no room for them. In order to make them feel welcome the Indian government has gone out of its way to give them jobs. The Vice-President of India is a Muslim, and there are at least as many Muslim ambassadors and ministers as merit warrants; other things being reasonably equal Muslims are given preferential recruitment for posts in the All-India Services. However, in the states of Uttar Pradesh and Madhya Pradesh where they used to be the dominant minority there is sometimes trouble when they find it difficult to reconcile themselves to behaving like a minority and one of them kills a cow, which Hindus hold sacred, or shows disrespect to a Hindu woman. So long as they flaunt their neighbours' feelings the government will not be able to protect them from the consequences. However, the proof that they are treated as full citizens lies in the fact that over a million Muslims who ran away to East Pakistan when riots broke out in Bengal in 1950 have returned to India and that there has since been an exodus of Muslims from East Pakistan into Assam and West Bengal on such a scale that the Indian government has had to begin deporting them back to Pakistan despite repeated diplomatic protests from Pakistan. However, in West Bengal communal harmony is only skin deep because of the way in which the Hindu minority is treated in East Pakistan. Whenever Hindu refugees come pouring into Calcutta with tales of horror about the way they are treated in East Pakistan there is a reaction. There were severe communal riots in both Bengals in 1950 and again in 1964. In each case the trouble started in East Pakistan where the government treats its Hindus as second-class citizens. So long as there are Hindus in East Pakistan – there are practically none left in West Pakistan – the status of India's Muslims cannot be finally settled. Hindus are very tolerant, but if the remaining nine million Hindus of East Bengal were to flood into India, Hindu tolerance might be tested beyond endurance, and pressure might be brought to bear on Muslims to migrate to Pakistan and make room for the newcomers. That this is something to be considered by Pakistan in her relations with India was shown in 1964 when, for the first time since Partition, more Muslims were killed in India than Hindus in Pakistan.

CHRISTIANS

There are 11 million Christians in India. The history of Christianity in India goes back 19 centuries to the time when the Apostle Thomas landed in south India where he remained till the end of his life. The majority of the Christians, however, are Roman Catholics who were converted by the Portuguese sometimes forcibly in the sixteenth and seventeenth centuries. The Roman Catholics continue, despite centuries of conversion, to marry within their own original castes; they are often found in the big cities, particularly Bombay. In eastern India they are predominantly members of the professional and skilled classes. In western India, however, Roman Catholics are often still very poor and backward. In Kerala, for example, those of Untouchable origin are confined to Untouchable benches in church. This is an absolute violation of Christ's teaching.

The Protestants are mostly found in backward tribal areas or amongst Untouchables. There are in addition over 100,000 Protestant Anglo-Indians, descended from British fathers, usually soldiers, planters or petty officials. One seat is reserved for them in Parliament. At the time of Independence many Anglo-Indians claimed British nationality and migrated to Britain and the old Dominions where they have been assimilated without trouble. The 100,000 who opted for Indian nationality have done very well; they are the backbone of the railways, the postal services, nursing and higher secretarial work; their knowledge of English, their mother tongue, made them a middle-class *élite* and now that the British have gone and they behave like Indians the stigma of being half-caste has gone also. Understandably, however, Anglo-Indians to do well have to forget that their fathers used to be the rulers of India.

Christians are full members of Indian society, but the Indian government frowns on proselytization and is making it more and more difficult for foreign missionaries to operate in India unless they confine their activities to teaching and healing. Since Hinduism is a non-proselytizing religion, this restriction is understandable. Gandhi once wrote: 'No propaganda can be allowed which reviles other religions, particularly when the reviling is done by foreigners.'

THE SIKHS

The next biggest minority group consists of eight million Sikhs. The Sikhs are a martial Hindu brotherhood. They originate from the Punjab where they were set up against the Muslims in the sixteenth century by Guru Nanak their leader. They are famous for their superb physique, their magnificent war record, their beards, their turbans and their prowess in agriculture and petty engineering.

They were badly hit by the partition of India which gave most of their irrigated lands to Pakistan and caused many of them to become refugees. But they lost no time in developing what land they received on the Indian side of the border, and those who could not get land are providing the whole of India with her taxi drivers, electricians, tailors and fortune-tellers.

THE BUDDHISTS
India gave Buddhism to the world 2,500 years ago, which then faded away from the land of its birth. At the time of Independence in 1947 there were only 200,000 Buddhists left in India. But in 1956 three million Untouchables from Maharashtra and Madhya Pradesh changed over to Buddhism at the instance of Dr Ambedkar, their leader, who died soon after. Whether these conversions are genuine is too early to say. So far it looks as if these Untouchables are using Buddhism primarily in order to overcome their social disabilities; however, since conversion deprives them of their special privileges under the Constitution, they may find it more profitable to revert to Hinduism.

THE JAINS
The Jains, who number about two million, are concentrated on the west coast; they engage mainly in trade and belong to a Hindu heresy. They are vegetarians and so loath to take life that they do not eat anything that has to be pulled out of the ground. Like the Sikhs, they intermarry with Hindus.

THE PARSIS
The Parsis are Zoroastrians who fled from Persia in the seventh century. They settled near Bombay and part of their religion is a symbolic worship of fire. Their contribution to Indian development is totally disproportionate to their numbers; there are only 115,000 of them, but they are very prominent in industry. For example, the greatest of all the Indian industrial houses, Tatas, is Parsi. They have also played a very significant role in Congress politics and in India's educational and scientific advance.

In addition to the religious minorities there are over 60 million Untouchables who are Hindus, but outside the caste structure. The government does a great deal for them; not only do they have 76 out of 506 seats reserved for them in Parliament, but they also have ministers at the Centre and in every state; in 1963 the Congress President himself was an Untouchable who had previously been chief minister of Andhra. Outside Hinduism altogether, there are the tribes scattered over remote jungle or hilly areas. Some practise animism, others are Hindu or Christian and they number perhaps 20 million. A certain number of these tribes are still at the Stone Age, like the Uralis of Kerala who hunt with bows and stones and live in the tops of trees surrounded by wild elephants. At the other extreme the Nagas of Assam run a hydro-electric station and have just been granted a state of their own.

Indian diversity is endless. It does not end with religion: it extends to caste and subcaste with the result that the whole of India is made up of minorities. Thus, the Brahmins never make up more than 11 per cent of the population in any one state; sometimes they make up 2 or 3 per cent, and even then are subdivided into sub-castes. The middle cultivating castes are often fairly evenly divided into watertight groups like the Lingayats and the Vokaligas of Mysore who worship different deities; or like the Kammas and the Reddys of Andhra. Therefore, in a way, to belong to a minority group in India is the rule rather than the exception. In a land where the social fabric is made up of so many minorities, the government must indeed be solicitous for the feelings of the minorities.

52 The means of communication with the outside world for families such as this one at a village in Orissa are still fairly primitive.

53 But in the towns radio, news-papers and Western influence are in evidence.

54 The Constitution stipulates free compulsory education for all children up to the age of fourteen. At a village primary school in 1957.

55 This modern junior secondary school at Chandigarh was designed by Pierre Jeanneret as part of Le Corbusier's plan for the town in the 1950s.

56 Education centres for adults have developed, such as this one at Madras.

57 As well as being rehabilitated refugees are also provided with their own education centres. This is at Calcutta.

58 (*left*) The first general election on universal adult franchise was held in 1951–2. Because of illiteracy, symbols were used to represent political parties.

59 (*below left*) Campaigning in Rajasthan during the election.

60 (*top right*) Indians love voting, and elections have become part of their life. A queue of men voters in Calcutta during the 1962 election.

61 (*centre right*) Voters receiving their ballot papers.

62 (*below right*) Muslim and Hindu women voters.

63 The tribal and the classical dance have long been part of India's culture. These women of the Santhal tribe in east India dance to celebrate spring.

64 The tribal dance is a form of religious ritual in which dancer and spectator participate. These dancers and musicians are from Hyderabad.

65 The classical dance has developed into a sophisticated art-form. This Manipuri or circular dance symbolizes the union of individual souls with the Supreme Soul.

66 The Kathakali is a dance drama which portrays stories from the *Ramayana* and *Mahabharata*. It originated in Kerala.

67 Vinoba Bhave, Gandhi's spiritual heir, quenched the communist guerrilla war in Hyderabad by appealing to the landed to give land to the landless.

68 The political situation in the state of Kerala where there is a strong Communist Party has necessitated the promulgation of President's Rule on three occasions. A communist demonstration at New Delhi in 1959.

8   Equality and Social Change

GANDHI STARTED HIS STRUGGLE for freedom because he wanted to make all Indians equal; his two major concerns were the abolition of untouchability and the emancipation of women. In 1924 he wrote:

> Untouchability is the sin of the Hindus. They must suffer for it, they must purify themselves, they must pay the debt they owe to their suppressed brothers and sisters. Theirs is the shame and theirs must be the glory when they have purged themselves of the black sin. All reform to be sincere and lasting must come from within.

Gandhi was of course right; all that legislation can do is to provide opportunities for those who are sufficiently educated to know that the law is on their side. What the government has done for the Untouchables has already been dealt with on page 135. But what is happening to them in fact?

In the cities the legislation has taken its full effect. Nobody discriminates against Untouchables; it is too dangerous because the law punishes the offender. In the villages, however, the position is very different. To begin with, those Untouchables who have become educated migrate to the town so that, with the exception of those who get jobs as village teachers, the untouchable *élite* is not there to help their kin to exert their newly acquired rights. In any case the Untouchables in the village are usually dependent on their caste neighbours for their livelihood since they seldom own land and have to obtain employment in the village. This means they dare not

145

draw water from the public well or enter the village temple as it would be slapping their patrons in the face. However, when they go to another village where nobody knows them they often behave like everybody else, take water from public wells and visit the temple if they feel so inclined. From time to time there is tension; violence sometimes flares up when they try to exert their rights in their own village. Thus, for instance, in the very orthodox state of Madras there practically was a civil war in 1957 when the Untouchables of the district of Ramnathapuram decided to vote for their own candidate instead of the candidate their caste patrons had told them to vote for. The fact that Untouchables had used their own political judgement so enraged the caste villagers that they set fire to the Untouchable villages; the Untouchables retaliated and the government backed them. The caste leader, a member of Parliament, was tried and sent to jail. The caste villagers of Ramnathapuram have learnt their lesson: in the 1962 elections there was no further trouble when the Untouchables voted as they pleased.

Sometimes, too, in a village it happens that an Untouchable gets into trouble, perhaps because his new prosperity has made him enemies, or because he visited the temple at the instigation of some local politician. If called, the police side with the Untouchable because that is the law; but if the victim is dependent on village goodwill, it is better for him to leave the village for nobody will give him work.

Where the Untouchables are economically independent of their caste neighbours they have been able to improve their social status by what has been described as Sanskritization. The most successful case of Sanskritization has taken place in parts of Uttar Pradesh where the Chamar caste of Untouchables is both numerically fairly large, so that it has political power, and economically independent. These Chamars, unlike most Untouchables, own enough land not to have to work for others. They now call themselves Thakurs; they no longer eat meat, work leather or touch dead animals. Today they marry their daughters off in their earliest teens for dowries instead of in their late teens for love. Gradually they are becoming accepted as belonging to a clean caste, although nobody of a caste higher than theirs would in fact eat with them, let alone marry into their group. What the Chamars have gained is somewhat intangible. They have managed to squeeze their own group up one step in the hierarchical ladder of caste; this may mean that from now on they will be allowed a couple of feet nearer the deity, or will be permitted to sit a few inches further forward at feasts on those occasions when the whole village worships or eats. Such occasions are formal and few but important because it is then that each group and sub-group's exact ranking in the warrant of caste precedent becomes of paramount and visually demonstrable importance.

It will take a very long time before untouchability is eradicated from the villages. Moreover, the Untouchables are not in a position to take full advantage of the urbanization which is sweeping India so long as they remain unskilled. Life for them is still kinder in the village because even if they have no land, they at least have a roof they can call their own, no matter how inadequate, and this often keeps them in the village, for even a hovel is better than the side-walks of the big city.

Perhaps the most useful of all the provisions in favour of the Untouchables are those concerning education. Only by becoming educated can the Untouchables overcome their economic dis-abilities and those who have become aware of this fact are very keen on sending their children to school. For those who have not realized this, there is very little the government can do.

The privileges extended to the Harijans – as the Untouchables are officially called – have turned caste upside down. There are so many advantages to having one's caste entered upon the Schedule that in the extreme case of the state of Mysore, 75 per cent of the population has insisted on being treated as Backward in order to get easier admission to university and more government jobs. The result has been to exclude the Brahmins – the most advanced caste – who find it so difficult to get university admission and government jobs, not only in Mysore but also in the rest of south India, that they tend to migrate north and to the big cities where universities are still open to talent and where the central government and private employers are still looking for people who can use their minds. In this way, the dispossessed Brahmins of south India are being pushed to the van-guard of modernization, and whether it is as journalists, account executives, managers, engineers, civil servants or planners they are still fulfilling their ancient destiny as leaders; but now they are leaders of change.

About the emancipation of women, Gandhi wrote: 'I am un-compromising in the matter of women's rights. In my opinion she should harbour under no legal disability not suffered by man. I should treat the daughters and the sons on a footing of perfect equality.' While he was alive he took great care to involve women in politics, sending them to picket and to jail just as if they were men. His reasons were many, and three of them were crucial. First, he wanted to make sure that women would become active participants in the building of the nation and in fighting for their own due. Secondly, he realized that if the women were not involved in the struggle for freedom they would prevent the men from joining. Thirdly, Gandhi had never forgotten both that women are half a country's population and that in India women are far more courage-ous than men. For example, it was Gandhi's mother who had sent him to England against the wishes of the caste elders, and it was Nehru's wife who encouraged him to follow Gandhi against paternal orders.

Hindu women have always been much respected, but through the centuries the respect was so great that they became over-protected and were deprived of all civic rights. The reason behind this is that in theory a woman was always some male relative's ward. Until she married a woman was the responsibility of her father, on marriage she became the responsibility of her husband, on his death that of his family. This has been changed by law. The new Hindu Code gives them almost full equality with men. Monogamy has been enforced for Hindus (Muslims are still allowed four wives under Quranic law), and divorce is now permitted for much the same causes as in Britain. Daughters now inherit an equal share with their brothers, inherit their husband's estate on his death, and are given the guardian-ship of their children. Of these reforms the most revolutionary is the daughters' right to inherit for this is a right the bridegroom's family has a stake in seeing observed.

Perhaps even more than the law, it is education which is going to emancipate women most. Women are taking to education with enthusiasm. In 1960 there were 200,000 girls at university whereas in 1900 there were only half a dozen. In the villages also, more and more girls are going to school. Indeed, literate wives have become status symbols for middle-class husbands, so that many prosperous villagers send their daughters to school in the hope that they will get richer husbands and require smaller dowries. Education plays a tremendous part in female emancipation. Once a girl has been to school she becomes more demanding and exercises more freely the right of veto she has always had when it comes to accepting a husband. The extreme cases, of course, are to be found in the towns where the age of marriage has gone up considerably and where girls often work and continue to work after they are married. There is no dearth of jobs for educated girls. India is crying out for teachers, nurses, demonstrators, typists. In government service a slight preference is given to women, as indeed it is in the choice of candidates for seats in Parliament and State Assemblies.

The Congress Party makes a point of reserving 15 per cent of its tickets for women, and this forces the other parties to sponsor women also. There are women ministers in each state and there are women Vice-Chancellors of universities, women State Governors, and even a woman Chief Minister in one state.[16] In the administrative services women have risen to responsible positions like District Collectors; there is a woman doctor who is a Squadron-Leader in the para-troopers; another woman is the Trade Union leader of the Calcutta dock-workers. If one counts them all, from teachers to administrators, from typists to nurses, there are perhaps half a million women in government service.

Women in India did not have to fight for their position, this was done for them by Mahatma Gandhi when he insisted on taking them with him into the struggle against British rule. Nehru once said that if he had to choose between educating only boys or only girls, he would educate the girls because they will be the mothers and will educate their children. Nehru realized that nothing holds society back as much as uneducated grandmothers, particularly in a society where they have so much to do with the arranging of marriages so that progress can only take place at the pace acceptable to its oldest and most conservative section.

The social changes that have taken place in India since 1947 as a result of government initiative must be seen in the light of Congress promises during the days of struggle. However, change has not been confined to government's blueprints and much of the change that is pulling the fabric of India's age-old society has been the indirect result of what has been happening at the political and economic levels.

Those who knew India before Independence cannot fail to be profoundly impressed by both the direct and the indirect changes that are taking place.

There has been a striking shift away from orthodoxy amongst Hindus. This shift has not been brought about by any deliberate government action but by the very fact of Independence. Orthodoxy is losing ground every day as more people become educated, as they go to the cities where they mix with people of all sorts and earn their livelihood through jobs hitherto reserved for certain castes. Brahmins are going into industry and the navy while Untouchables become school teachers and government officials. Education, industrialization and urbanization are the great destroyers of orthodoxy just as improved communications and the spread of literacy are the great promoters of faith.

In the past it took months to go on pilgrimage at the slow pace of the bullock cart; today it is both quick and cheap because the government runs cheap pilgrim trains. In the past one had to be literate to read the *Ramayana* or the *Gita*, or wait for a passing minstrel to visit the village; today one switches on the radio to listen to devotional songs or the Scriptures, and the cinema devotes most of its mileage to religious subjects. Between them, the radio and the cinema have done for Hinduism what printing did for Christianity. And in addition there is of course printing itself, which now that so many more people can read brings to the villages the authoritative version in the vernacular of what had in the past been left to the fallible memory of itinerant priests or holy beggars. The radio has undermined the position of the priest in the village; at festival time one can now tune in to the right hymns and therefore the priests' bargaining power has diminished considerably. There has been the odd case where a gramophone record has replaced an extortionate Brahmin. In the more advanced areas there are priests who have become so aware of their plight that they send their sons to the city to become petrol pump attendants or office clerks for the orthodoxy on which they themselves thrived may not last their children's life-time. Already the income of the priest has been drastically hit by inflation whereas industrial wages keep pace with the cost of living. If people give less to the priest it is not because they have lost faith but because the priest only plays a menial part in Hinduism and they are becoming less orthodox and therefore less prone to fear the evil eye; thus if there is an epidemic of smallpox, more and more people get themselves inoculated instead of giving alms to the priest.

At the same time people are becoming more religious. Under the British, many a modern educated Indian took care to hide the fact that he and his wife performed puja. For holidays, they visited Europe like the typical British family. Today nobody makes a secret of praying and, perhaps thanks to restrictions on foreign travel due to the shortage of foreign exchange, it has become fashionable to travel in India so that most people take a quite new-found pride in going from pilgrimage centre to pilgrimage centre as tourists-cum-devotees. The young *élite* is firmly modern, but it is also firmly Hindu. They look on Sanskrit, for instance, as Westerners might look on Latin, an interesting discipline, but no longer a way of thought. As a result more people learn Sanskrit than ever before, yet Sanskrit plays little part in their lives. However, their whole way of looking at life is coloured by Hindu thought; they have a serene confidence that Hinduism, purged of its bigotry, is one of the great religions of the world.

With the breakdown of the belief in ritual, other institutions are also disappearing. Amongst these is the joint-family system. Under this system all the married sons and grandsons, together with their children, remained under the paternal roof. They all shared the family income and obeyed their elders, particularly the older women and the oldest man. This system which was prevalent above all amongst the richer members of society – the merchants, the land/lords and the bigger peasants – has been undermined by a series of factors.

First, the economic factors. Taxation in India makes a negligible allowance for dependents, and now that it is very high, indeed penal on higher incomes, the rich have every incentive to split up their assets by partitioning the joint family. Furthermore, once the sons have got their share and live separately, the hold of the joint family on them disappears with astonishing rapidity. Another incentive to the partition of the land is provided by land reforms with their drastic ceilings on the amount an individual family can keep (see Land reforms, pages 155–8).

However, in a country as poor as India the economic factors which undermine the joint/family system only affect a fraction of the population; there are other factors which affect the majority.

Education is one of them. Once wives are educated they become reluctant to kow/tow to their illiterate mother/in/law. The moment they give birth to a son, and thus gain their husband's support, they insist on setting/up house on their own, even if that house is but an extension of the family hut with a separate kitchen and an all/purpose room. The consciousness of the market and its price mechanism which came to so many Indian villages during the Second World War is another factor. Once the peasant ceases to be self/sufficient and begins to look at his income in terms of cash rather than kind, he begins to want to save, or spend in the way he likes. One cannot do anything else but store grain or barter it, so one does not really mind pooling the grain in the family silo and taking out whatever everybody needs. Money somehow has an attraction of its own; and there is room for endless quarrels if one member of the family takes more out of the reserves than the others, because while there is a limit to how much a man can eat there is no limit to how much he can spend.

Urbanization is another factor. Once the son goes to town to work he becomes reluctant to send all he can save to the family, particularly if his earnings have to carry idle nephews or ailing brothers. Moreover, living in cities is not like living in the village where one can always add one room or sleep out; urban houses and flats are not elastic. Overcrowding often breaks up the joint family. And the very poor, those who have nothing to share, were never part of the joint family, because everybody always has to fend for themselves. Therefore the joint-family system which made Indian society so medieval is being replaced by the modern system of restricting the family to the husband, the wife, their children and perhaps a widowed mother who finds in her son's home the social security which the Indian government does not provide.

The breakdown of the joint-family system is both a good and a bad thing. It is a good thing because it frees the enterprising and the modern-minded from bondage; the improvident and the idle can no longer flourish at industrious relatives' expense. But it is also a bad thing because there is no provision in India for the sick or the unemployed.

A further change since Gandhi came onto the Indian scene has been the influences which have affected the caste system. The changes may not be spectacular but they are nevertheless drastic.

Caste has been affected by a combination of forces which conspire to undermine the established hierarchy. Indian villagers often describe what is happening by saying 'a wind is blowing' because although they have noticed the changes, they are not clear about the causes.

As a result of this 'wind', caste councils have given up the practice of formal excommunication. In the old days when somebody had been excommunicated the caste council sent a circular to all the members of the caste – or the subcaste – to inform them of the risks they would run if they ate or took water from the pariah. Now, with greater mobility, greater opportunity of employment in town, this has been given up. The caste council may still boycott the culprit within the village, and make it difficult for him to find a wife from his own community, but it no longer bothers to inform all and sundry nor does the boycott means celibacy any more (there are so many widows one can marry, moreover one can even marry out of caste without having to give up one's religion as one had to under the British). The caste councils are realizing that they can only weaken their authority by going against the tide;[17] therefore, they reserve formal excommunication for those crimes for which they know they will have the full support of public opinion. Thus, nobody takes notice of people going abroad any more, or of Brahmins serving in the navy. Yet barely half a century ago Gandhi, not even a Brahmin, was excommunicated because he crossed the ocean.

Amongst the winds which blow upon caste is the economic factor. People have to work in order to survive. Slowly, surely, caste is being eroded by work. One can find Brahmins who cultivate their own farm with their own hands – an occupation which, except for the Anavil Brahmins of Gujerat and certain hillBrahmins of Uttar Pradesh, used to be taboo. In Bengal there is an increasing number of uppercaste Hindus working in factories as unskilled labourers – polluting themselves by contact with the other workers. The most remarkable case of caste breaking known to the author is that of a caste villager in ultraorthodox Tanjore who worked as a sweeper for an American anthropologist visiting his village.

The most immediate and important factors, however, which have affected caste are politics and land reforms.

Before Gandhi, leadership was with the top castes, above all the Brahmins. Tilak, Gokhale, and Ram Mohan Roy were all Brahmins. As late as 1945 nobody could have foretold that it would be a positive handicap to be a Brahmin. Gandhi dynamited the entire caste hierarchy when he insisted on taking the people with him into politics; a decision which was embodied at Independence in the policy which gives each adult one vote, irrespective of caste, creed, resources or education.

Elections have taken power away from the Brahmins who are a tiny minority everywhere; in most states they cannot get themselves elected any more. The Untouchables, never more than 30 per cent of the population in any one place, can only become important if the majority group is divided so that they get the casting power of the

154

floating voter. However, in most states the cultivating castes form a sufficiently homogenous group to deprive the Untouchables of this bargaining power. The result is that the Untouchables, in order to be represented in politics, have to continue to rely upon the seats which are specially kept for them.

By contrast the middle cultivating castes, as well as the artisan and craftsmen castes have been revolutionized by politics. Power can only be had if enough votes are pooled together so that the old premium on being different – higher and better than people almost like oneself – has been replaced by the new premium of being alike. As a result the subcastes are gradually blurring, subcaste names are dropped, the taboos begin to disappear between members of the dominant cultivating caste and the artisan caste of an area, as they all coalesce back into one main caste. Thus in Maharashtra the Marathas who are the dominant cultivating caste no longer call themselves Maratha Kumbis, etc., but Marathas. They now inter׳dine, and are even beginning to arrange marriages across the old subcaste boundaries and they accept as equals certain artisan groups like the oil׳pressers and the goldsmiths. It is only a matter of time before the Indian social structure becomes like a sandwich with a thick middle caste filling between two thin layers of bread: the Brahmins above and the Untouchables below. Nobody will coalesce with them, the Brahmins because nobody is likely to forget their traditional position, the Untouchables because they are too polluting. The risk is that, as this caste sandwich takes shape, the rigour with which society kept the subcastes pure will be applied to this new three׳tier caste structure. There would then be three castes instead of many; but it would still be a caste society.

It is an interesting footnote to what is happening that after the 1962 elections no Brahmin minister was appointed in Andhra, Kerala, Gujerat, or the Punjab; in Andhra there were five Reddy Ministers in a cabinet of nine, and in the Punjab five Sikh Ministers in a cabinet of eight.

A further factor which has had a profound effect on caste has been land reform. Although this was not on Gandhi's programme, it has been a major Congress objective since 1931. It has also gone a long way to undermine the upper castes and strengthen the middle peasant castes.

Before 1947 much of the land was owned by the upper castes. In northern India the *zemindars* and *jagirdars* (landlords or alienees of the land revenue or both) were Rajputs, while everywhere in India the Brahmins had a good deal of land. In Tanjore, for instance, most of the rice land was owned by Brahmins. All over India, too, much land had passed into the hands of moneylenders, nearly all of whom belong to a few trading castes. While much of the land was thus held by the upper castes, the rest was in the hands of the middle agricultural castes who are the backbone of the independent peasantry.

Since Independence there have been many land reforms; well over 200 Acts have been passed in the states (land reform is not a federal subject). The basis of all Indian land reform is the simple slogan 'land to the tiller'. The methods of giving land to the tiller vary from state to state, but a few features are common to all the states.

In giving land to the tiller the first step was the abolition of feudal jurisdiction and the buying out of the alienees of the land revenue; the only thing which varied from state to state was the price at which they were bought out and how much of it was in cash or in non-convertible bonds. The size of the compensation was in inverse proportion to the size of the land which was being taken away, from 20 times the net income for small men to three times for big men. And in the special case of Rajasthan, where the feudal landlords were politically powerful and desperate enough to turn bandit in protest, the compensation had eventually to be raised to restore law and order.

The tenants were already protected from eviction under pre-war land reforms, so all that happened once they were freed from the obligation to pay their rent to the alienee of the land revenue was that they paid it to the government direct. The change was both good and bad. Bad because government is much more impersonal and less willing to suspend payment when a calamity has occurred which does not fall within one of those for which remission of land revenue is indicated, like a failure of the crop or a flood. Good because tenants have been freed from the obligation to bribe the landlord's agent, to pay an illegal cess when the landlord, or his agent, have a daughter to marry or a son to educate, and they are at last allowed to buy the land which they cultivate. Under the new reforms tenants are either allowed or compelled – this varies from state to state – to buy out their landlord. As far as the landlords are concerned, in all states they have been allowed to take back some land from their tenants on condition that they will cultivate the land themselves – with the help of farm labourers – provided the amount of land they are left with does not exceed the ceiling.

All over India ceilings on the amount of land a family can own have been introduced; only orchards and plantations are exempt. The ceiling is usually set at 16 acres of wet land and for un, irrigated land it ranges from 30 to 50 acres. There has been some evasion of land reforms. In anticipation of the ceiling most land, owners divided their land amongst the members of their family, or evicted their tenants illegally by keeping land off their records. Nevertheless, by and large the reforms have made considerable changes in the villages. The days when a man's land extended over square miles are over. The small absentee landlord who has been allowed to keep his land often can no longer collect his rent; but the man who himself farms anything up to 50 acres has usually managed to remain untouched, while the landlord who lives in the village has often managed to make his tenants continue to pay the old rent. Paradoxically, however, the poor peasant, the man with less than two acres on rent, has been hardest hit by land reforms. He has to work as a labourer to make both ends meet and the result of land reforms is that his lease has been terminated by the owner who cultivates the land himself in order not to lose it, while the splitting up of holdings means that people no longer require as many hired hands.

It is undoubtedly upon the upper castes that the effect of land reform has been most drastic. The Brahmin, the Rajput, the money, lender have lost their estates with the result that they no longer matter so much in the village. Those who have gained are the middle agricultural castes who have bought a great deal of land from the castes above them, and who now do much of their cultivation them-selves. Moreover, land reforms have strengthened the middle caste by introducing economic equality. Peasants have split up their holdings between their relations and their caste fellows to avoid ceilings. A man who owns square miles of land cannot find enough relatives or caste fellows in his village to divide his land; but the middle peasant with perhaps a hundred acres of land can – in order to avoid the ceiling which is of the order of 16 acres of irrigated and 30 acres of dry land – by dividing it between his sons, nephews, friends. And they of course are all of his own caste.

Land reforms have been very effective in splitting up the land, but they have failed to raise the underdog, the Untouchable and the poor peasant who have not been able to acquire land. The Un-touchables and the landless remain backward even when the government gives them priority reclaimed wasteland. This is because they have neither the capital nor the know-how to make the land prosper.

The government's efforts to help the villagers also tend to strengthen the main peasant castes. For instance, the Community Project's Extension approach by which improved methods of cultivation are brought to the villagers strengthens them because it is they who have the land with which to get the benefits. Loans for tube wells will be given only to men with enough land to be able to make use of the tube well; new crops can be tried only by those peasants with enough land to spare after they have sown the food crops which they need for themselves. The government has invested a great amount of money in co-operative loans; but since these loans are only given to the credit-worthy with enough surety for the co-operative to feel its money will be recovered, only the better-off peasants can apply for them. Much of the same thing happens in the case of village and district self-government, Panchayati Raj as it is called, which the government is sponsoring to improve life in the villages. The main beneficiaries are the peasants of the dominant castes who have been given yet another opportunity for exercising economic as well as political patronage.

To sum up, in the villages there has been a great deal of social change, particularly in the more traditional and private spheres of family life, but village organization has so far changed very little; except that the very rich have ceased to exist; that some Brahmins have taken to cultivating their land themselves in order not to lose it; and that the very poor may be getting poorer. The only real change is that power has slipped from the hands of the few big men in the village to a large number of medium ones. This shift has, if anything, had the result of strengthening the position of the middle castes.

69 India's agriculture is subsistence agriculture and the average peasant grows just enough rice on which to live. Rice being transplanted in Madras.

70 Tea is the most important and largest earner of foreign exchange. A tea picker in Assam.

71 Primitive methods of cultivation such as the wooden plough are still commonly used. This Muslim peasant is from Uttah Pradesh.

72 Because the Hindu believes the cow to be sacred, cattle and people compete for subsistence. This is at Polumbakan in Madras.

73 In Kashmir rice is cultivated in terraced fields.

74 Land reform which has been a major objective since 1931 is gradually ridding India of her powerful landlords. A landlord and tenant farmer in the Punjab.

75 (*below*) About one peasant in two is in debt to the moneylender.

76 Five-sixths of India's population live in villages such as this one in Orissa.

77 This village is for Untouchables who are outside the caste system and whose status Gandhi tried to improve.

78 A co-operative organization sponsored by a group of Gandhian followers helps to provide extra food for the peasants. Here a peasant receives a measure of rice.

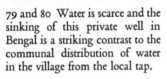

79 and 80 Water is scarce and the sinking of this private well in Bengal is a striking contrast to the communal distribution of water in the village from the local tap.

81 The peasant's crops depend on primitive irrigation methods such as these.

82 The government helps to combat disease amongst children by establishing health centres such as this one.

83 Women social village workers being assembled for a course of instruction.

84 (*above*) These women are picking cotton, which has long been one of India's principal crops.

85 Mats made from coir rope, the outer husk of the coconut, is an important industry for the state of Kerala.

9   Agriculture and Poverty

INDIA IS A COUNTRY OF PEASANTS; peasants so poor that their poverty passes the imagination of those who have never experienced it at first hand.

Five-sixths of India's 475,000,000 people live in villages; three out of four people depend upon agriculture for their livelihood. Most people in rural India own at least a tiny plot of land – perhaps just big enough to build a hut on – and four-fifths of the people who earn their living from the land own some of it; though half of them do not own more than perhaps half an acre, and many of them own much less. The number of people who own a substantial amount of land is very small; indeed, if all the land in excess of 30 acres was confiscated it would affect hardly ten per cent of the agricultural land. The average Indian family holding is five acres for a family of four. This, compared with Western farming, means poverty. Yet, in India five acres of land is a relatively large amount and the owner of it, especially if the five acres have enough water for him not to be at the mercy of the vagaries of the monsoon, is a respected citizen who carries much weight in his village. In India, poverty is made worse because yields are so low. Wheat yields are a third of what they are in Britain; rice yields are a third of what they are in Japan.

India's agriculture is a subsistence agriculture. With so little land and such low yields it is almost inevitable that the farmer has to grow food for himself, for his family and for his animals. The family eats the grains, the animals eat the stalks which are left over from the thatching of the family roof. Only one-third of India's cereals ever comes to the market, the rest is consumed on the spot. This need to provide for the family pot means that land cannot always be put to the most economic use; the farmer who could grow cotton or groundnuts often plants millets instead, because he has not got enough land to provide for his food as well as for the market.

With inefficient subsistence farming of this kind India must be poor. The average income per person is about £27 a year. Many people in the villages have often only four or five shillings per head per week. People in small towns are somewhat more prosperous; people in the big cities are a great deal more prosperous and they have incomes over twice the national average. It has been calculated by the Indian government that in 1963 270,000,000 people had no more than eight pence per day and that, if all goes well, at the end of the Ninth Five-Year Plan, by 1996 there will still be 258,000,000 Indians out of the anticipated population of 850,000,000 who will have less than ten shillings a week.

The reason for the small size of holdings is threefold.

First, there is the terrific pressure of population on the land. Until after the First World War India's population grew slowly. In 1921 India had not much more than half as many people as it had in 1961. But, in the last twenty years the pace of growth has increased, and now the population increase is probably 2½ per cent per annum – perhaps 12,000,000 people. Before 1900 the increase was absorbed on the land without intolerable hardship because in many parts of India there was still some empty land to bring under the plough. But nowadays there is practically no land which can be brought under cultivation without very expensive improvements, either irrigation or reclamation from erosion or deep-rooted weeds.

Secondly, the size of holdings has been affected by Hindu and Muslim law both of which entitle each son to a share of the family land. To make fragmentation worse, the sons usually insist on getting a share of each type of land. Thus if a farmer has four sons and four acres of land, not only will each son get one acre, but each son will get his acre in bits to make sure that he gets one-quarter of the land near the well, one-quarter of the land on which cotton can grow, one-quarter of the land under rice, etc. So that by the time the land has been divided and subdivided over a few generations, it is usual for one man's farm to be scattered over a dozen or more plots,

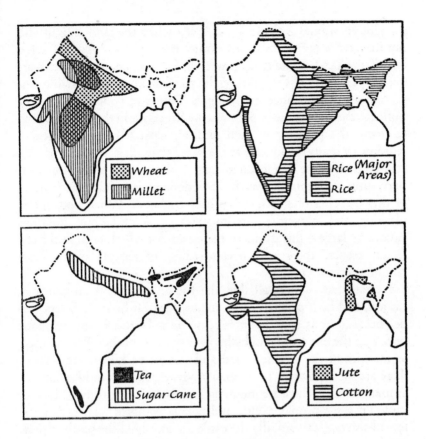

Maps showing distribution of principal crops

some the size of a flower bed. Under such conditions, the sensible thing would be for some of the heirs to sell their share to the others and migrate to the city but so great is the prestige which attaches to the ownership of land and so few are the good jobs in the city that this is only done as a last resort. Fragmentation therefore adds to the inefficiency of Indian agriculture. In some states the government has now made the consolidation of holdings compulsory.

The third reason for which the fields are so small is that Indian techniques of cultivation are labour intensive. Over most of India the plough animal is the bullock. Even when the land is light and not irrigated a pair of bullocks cannot manage more than 15 acres; and if the land is heavy and wet, as for rice, many bullocks are needed. In parts of the south eight pairs of bullocks drawing one plough are not an uncommon sight. This is of course because the bullocks themselves are of poor quality. In addition the transplanting of rice – the planting of each seedling separately into the field – requires so many hands, all at the same time, that a family usually restricts itself to the area it can manage without hired help. Moreover, harvesting of cereals all over India is done with a sickle, each stalk, or tiny bunches of stalks, being held by hand. When both transplanting and harvesting are so extravagant of labour, holdings cannot be large – this is indeed the reason for which even in the old feudal estates, there was overcrowding of tenants or landless labourers on the land.

Nevertheless, despite all this, the Indian peasant is an expert at his job, and he is quite receptive to new ideas. If he is inefficient it is not because he is stupid but because he is bound by his religious beliefs on the one hand and by his poverty on the other. For instance, to the Hindu the cow is sacred and cannot be killed. As a result there are more cows in India than anywhere in the world; relatively as many cows as there are motor cars in America, with two heads of cattle for three people. Cattle and people compete with each other for subsistence, so naturally the cattle are mostly of the scrub variety. Many cows give no milk at all, many bullocks are too weak to work. India's milk production is the lowest in the world; the best cows yield only one-third of the milk in the West and the average Indian cows one-sixteenth. The peasant has begun only recently to use improved seeds. Seed farms are very new and there are not enough of them yet to make much difference, although there is a crying demand for better seeds. India has less fuel wood and timber per square mile of forest than anywhere in the world and much of the forest is inaccessible and coal is expensive; so the villagers have to burn cowdung with the result that there is not enough fertilizer to enrich the soil. The fact that there is a very thriving black market in fertilizer proves the peasants' willingness to use it. The black market is the result of shortages due to an inadequate fertilizer production programme under the five-year plans. Because he has to feed himself and his family the Indian peasant cannot rotate his crops, so that cereals which are very exhaustive have been grown for centuries on the same land, without any adequate replenishment of the soil.

The peasant's poverty is made the more crushing if he is a tenant or if he is in debt to the moneylender. Legal tenancy is no longer important but there is still a good deal of illegal crop-sharing, and the share of the peasant may then be half or sometimes even less than half the crop. About one peasant in two is in debt, and much of this debt is at rates of interest which run – again usually illegally – from 12 to 25 per cent of the crop. The debt position is being eased by the increasing amounts of money the government is pumping into the co-operative societies. The plan is that the societies will be lending £580 million by 1966; but even the societies usually lend at 9 per cent, and they are only supposed to lend for productive purposes, while much peasant borrowing in India is for weddings and funerals and thread ceremonies.[18] One of the most sacred duties for a father is to marry his daughter, to give her a dowry and a wedding feast, just as the first duty of a son is to bury his parents in style and to invite all the kin to the funeral feast. For this, the peasants have to borrow, and borrow until they have mortgaged their children's and their grandchildren's incomes, lest it be said that they are an un-natural son or father – in which case nobody will marry into their family. A wedding may well cost a year's income.

'To those that have shall be given' is nowhere truer than in village India. When the crop has been harvested the poorer peasants who have no staying power must sell some of their produce at the bottom of the market to pay their debts, their land revenue, as well as to purchase what they cannot themselves produce like salt, plough shares, kerosene or matches. It is only the better-off who can wait for prices to go up, before harvest when food or cash crops are in demand.

Not only his own poverty, but nature itself, seems to conspire against the Indian peasant. Much of India depends for water on the monsoon. Sometimes the monsoon fails, or is late, or is early, and sometimes, when it is on time it is too strong so that there are floods. Only where there is irrigation can the peasant feel reasonably certain that his crops will not fail for lack of water, though if the drought is too severe there may not be water in the catchment area, or it may have receded in the sub-soil table to a level beyond the reach of the tube wells, or if there is too much water, the irrigation canals may themselves lead to salinization and water logging. In any case three-quarters of India's land under cultivation is still entirely dependent on the rains since it is not under irrigation.

If Indian agriculture is to improve much has to be done. More knowledge and above all more money must be invested in the land. There must be enough improved seeds – which means enough seed farms – to go round, and the peasant must have enough money to improve his land. There must be more fertilizer and more fertilizer factories. There must be more artificial insemination centres and more veterinary surgeons, more stud bulls, more veterinary clinics, more fodder for the cattle and above all more water, which means more wells, more canals, more dams, and more money to pay for them all, especially since there usually occurs a gap in time between the provision and the utilization of canal irrigation, the costliest of all.

For agriculture to improve there has to be more money all round. This, however, in the vicious circle of India's poverty is not easy to provide. The bulk of the people are poor peasants who cannot be squeezed much more than they are squeezed already. The peasants spend four-fifths of their income on food and clothing, of which two-thirds goes on food grains which they often grow for themselves. Food, cloth, the compulsory ceremonies, direct taxes leave the peasant with very little for those items which pay indirect taxes – and which make up the bulk of the states revenue – such as kerosene, matches, sugar, soap, tea or coffee, or a train journey and a post-card to the relative in the town. Because the peasant is so poor his demands on the rest of the economy are negligible and that is why the rest of the economy is very small and why the government is so hard put to find the money it needs to pay for development.

Resources

The Congress government is committed to raising the standard of living and to economic equality. In 1947 the All-India Congress Committee declared:

> Political independence having been achieved, the Congress must address itself to the next great major task, viz. the establishment of real democracy in the country and a society based on social justice and equality. Such a society must provide every man and woman with equality of opportunity. This can only be realized when democracy extends from the political to the social and economic sphere.

However, economic equality cannot be brought about quickly in a country where the resources available are as limited as they are in India.

There is a railway network of 40,000 miles which makes a profit, because there are not enough roads or motor vehicles to compete effectively with it as is the case in most other countries in the world. There is a cotton textile industry – the second largest in the world – which produces more than 7,000 million yards of cloth a year (including handloom cloth), a jute industry – the largest in the world – which produces nearly one million tons of jute cloth a year, a steel industry which produces six million tons of steel a year. There is also a growing chemical and engineering industry but that is all. For a country of India's size and population it is very little indeed. All factory employment together adds up to perhaps 2 per cent of the total employment; industry does not matter outside the dozen places where it creates an island of modernity in the ocean of traditional peasant farming.

The infrastructure is not adequate, the railways cannot cope with the traffic thrust upon them; steel production has lagged behind because the railways could not move enough coal and coal mining was inadequate. Electric power, although it keeps doubling every five years, is only a fraction of what is available per head in the West and is in very short supply in India, where its inadequacy slows down industrial development. By the end of the Third Five-Year

175

Plan it is hoped that 50,000 out of India's 550,000 villages will have electricity. The road system is far from sufficient, and the roads are seldom bridged over major rivers. Only major roads are properly surfaced, so that lorries wear out much faster than in the West.

Taxes are so high that only in times of war have people in the West given so much to the state. The revenue of the Centre and the states together is now about 15 per cent of the national income, less than half the Western norm. In India necessities like soap and cooking-fat are taxed at rates thought suitable in the West only for semi-luxuries like cars and cosmetics. In India there are hardly any of the benefits of the welfare state except for factory workers and government servants. Hospitals are confined to the towns; the villagers only see a doctor when there is an epidemic or when they go to town for a serious illness. There is only one trained nurse to every 30,000 people. The better-off Indians are one of the most highly taxed people in the world. They pay income tax (with a steep built-in escalation), supertax, capital gains tax, wealth tax, gift tax, estate duty (the highest in the world after Ceylon) and an expenditure tax as well; and, if they are investors, all this is in addition to the very high taxes the companies have to pay on their profits.

By these extreme taxes the revenue has been raised to three times what it was in 1955. However, much of this increase has been swallowed up by the increase in defence expenditure caused by the Chinese threat. Defence expenditure is now over £600 million a year, well over three times as much as in 1955, and the armed forces have increased in number from 450,000 to about a million. Most of these are infantry and there is little modern equipment.

When the revenue of the Centre and the states added together only totals about £2 billion, development must come from savings and foreign aid.

In 1947 savings were perhaps 5 per cent of the national income, just enough to keep abreast of an increase in population of about 1½ per cent. Income per head in 1950 was probably about the same as in 1880. Savings grew in the 1950s but they are still no more than 10 per cent of the national income. And since most of it was invested at source, government could lay hands on a mere fraction of the savings. Indians are overwhelmingly self-employed and the self-employed tend, the world over, to plough their savings back into their avocations. Thus the peasant repairs his hut, replaces a bullock or a plough or digs a well, or eats better; the shopkeeper increases his stock; the artisan takes an apprentice. Even in industry the profits are ploughed back because that is one of the ways companies finance themselves; the other way of course is to raise money in the market. The government is therefore able to get only one-fifth of the savings either from the compulsory investment of provident funds in government securities, government banks and nationalized life insurance or from the sale of savings certificates.

The rest of the development has to be paid for by foreign aid. India gets foreign aid from a number of sources and so far the amounts have been going up. One of the forms in which foreign aid is given is the American Public Loan 480. Through this India gets wheat which is sold in India; the rupees received are then invested in various projects which have American approval and for which repayment is made in rupees. These rupees are then made available for the rupee expenditure of the American government in India, like payments to its staff in India and the costs of the Embassy. Other forms of aid are co-ordinated through the World Bank's Aid-India Club to which the International Monetary Fund and the Western nations who help India all belong and through the United Nations. Most of the aid is tied to particular projects and to supplies from the country of the donor. In 1961-2 India received £253 million, in 1962-3, £333 million, and in the first half of 1963-4, £200 million in aid. The amounts are creeping up, but India is not getting anything like her share of aid. At a time when the affluent countries are beginning to recognize their duty to help those less fortunate than themselves, India, on merit as well as performance, leaving aside the factors of population and size, should receive more than anybody else.

India needs more aid; she needs aid which is not tied to a particular project or to purchases from a particular country. Moreover, if aid is to be used to the maximum effect it ought to be given on a long enough basis to make planning possible; instead, it is doled out from fiscal year to fiscal year and delays combine with uncertainty to make it less and less effective.

Foreign aid is important twice over. It provides money for develop, ment. It also fills the gap in foreign exchange caused by the in, sufficiency of India's exports to pay for her imports. One of India's greatest difficulties is that her exports are inelastic. The biggest earner of foreign exchange is tea, but tea is mostly consumed in Britain and there is a limit to how many cups of tea even Britain can drink. Next to tea comes jute and jute goods, but the shift to bulk handling and the competition from East Pakistan is making it very difficult for India to export more of this commodity. Cotton textiles is another of India's exports but it is now hit by competition from Japan and there is a gentleman's agreement with Britain which is still trying to protect what is left of Lancashire, on how much cotton textile India may send. A new and promising line of export is iron and man, ganese ore, mainly to Japan, and sewing machines to the Common, wealth and the neighbouring countries; but this is not enough to earn the foreign exchange so vitally needed to make development possible. The rest has to come as foreign aid. Indians who make such heroic sacrifices to ensure a better future for their grandchildren should get more aid than one and a half dollars per head, especially when one stops to remember that along India's border lies the frontier of the free world.

10   Development and Planning

ONLY 17 PER CENT OF INDIA'S POPULATION, or 80 million people, live in towns of five thousand or more. The towns have been growing with mushroom rapidity, acting as a magnet for the educated and the skilled as well as for the landless peasants and the semi-skilled in search of something to do. In the ten years from 1951 to 1961 the population of Delhi and New Delhi put together went up by 70 per cent. Bombay has nearly doubled. Jamshedpur, the first of the steel towns, has more than doubled. There are now five cities with a population of more than one million. Calcutta, the second biggest city in the Commonwealth, has a population of 5½ million if one includes the suburbs. Bombay has over four million, Madras has nearly two million, and Hyderabad has 1¼ million people. In addition there are over a hundred cities with populations of over 100,000.

Urban growth has been accompanied by squalor and slums so shocking that the slum houses in England look like palaces by comparison. The misery of an Indian slum is impossible to imagine unless one has actually seen it with one's own eyes. People literally live, sleep, and die on the sidewalk. In the city of Calcutta, in the last census (1961), 19,000 people returned the pavement as their home but in fact many more than 19,000 live there; perhaps half a million or more sleep on the pavement year in year out, though they may have a cubby hole somewhere where they can store their scanty belongings during the day.

Some cities have grown because they already possessed the necessary infrastructure. This is particularly true of towns like Bombay, Calcutta, Asansol, Jamshedpur, Madras, Bangalore and

Delhi. Existing industry, existing facilities and the availability of skills on the spot always attract more industry. However, the government has done all it could to try and limit the growth of the existing towns in order to avoid congestion and above all in order to spread the benefits of industrialization as evenly as possible. Such a spread is politically wise even when it is economically wasteful. One of the methods the government has used is the control of the location of industry. This has prevented the concentration of all industry in the most efficient places; places near the sea, on major railway lines, and near raw materials, and places which already have skilled workers who do not have to be housed by the employer. As a result of this policy – the extreme instance of which was the location of a subsidiary refinery in Assam because the Assamese insisted that since they produced the oil, they had to be allowed to have a share of any industry it might produce – sleepy little towns have suddenly come to life. Bhopal, for instance, now has a large heavy electrical works. Poona, once the retreat of British colonels, is humming with industrial and educational activities from diesel pumps to a military academy; from a penicillin factory to machine tools. Finally, under government stimulus a whole series of totally new townships have sprung out of the jungle round totally new industries. The three government steel mills of Bhilai, Rourkela and Durgapur, for instance, are sprouting townships at meteoric pace. So are the fertilizer plants of Sindri and Nangal, and the locomotive plant of Chittaranjan. Once the jungle has been tamed; once roads have been built, railways laid, electricity and water provided; once a township has been built, the new town attracts other industries, particularly since the Indian plans favour the growth of industries in these new townships.

Planning came to India at the end of the war, quite naturally. For a long time the Congress Party had been planning-orientated. In the 1930s Pandit Nehru had headed a National Planning Committee which passed resolutions and issued reports at regular intervals. Planning had great appeal for Nehru on two counts. First, it was a Russian method of development and he had been profoundly impressed by the way in which the Russians had managed to become the world's second largest power, a success he attributed to planning – he seems to have swallowed whole the Western idea that the Russians were a backward and barbarian people in 1917, and did not realize how far Russia's industrial growth was the resumption of a process which had been interrupted, not started, in 1917. Secondly, Nehru instinctively saw in planning the modern way in which to develop India's resources, in sharp contrast to the Gandhian way of putting the village first and the state last. More/ over, by the end of the war planning had become fashionable. The British, too, had become plan minded; there was a Labour govern/ ment in Britain, with a planning programme of sorts; and in France there was the Monnet Plan. The atmosphere was in favour of planning, and the Congress Party was driven by the need to do something in office to make good those pledges they had been so prodigal with in opposition: that India would flow with milk and honey once colonial exploitation was ended. Faced with the need for immediate action the new government was thankful for the plans its British predecessor had made and for the blueprints which made it possible to start doing something at once. In some cases, indeed, the projects had already been started.

Formally, planning began in 1951 and we are now in the Third Five/Year Plan. Like the Soviet plans, the Indian plans are five/ year plans, but the resemblance ends there. The Indian plans are pragmatic, what Indians like to call 'elastic', by which they mean that the plan is for the people and not the people for the plan. If targets are not achieved in the planned period nobody is deported to the Andamans (the Indian equivalent of Siberia) let alone shot, the completion date is merely carried forward into the next plan period; and when necessary projects are dropped out of the plan, this is simply called 'fulfilling the core of the plan'. It is therefore possible to prune when circumstances demand without too much loss of face. There was some pruning in 1958 because of lack of foreign exchange, and in 1963 because of the Chinese aggression.

India's five/year plans are formulated within the framework of the Directive Principles of the Constitution. Their purpose is to ensure to the people of India adequate means of livelihood, the right to work, to education, and to some minimum standards of living. It was feared that without planned development the government would not be able to realize these objectives. The argument was that in an underdeveloped country, if there is to be a social content to political freedom, the initiative for development has to be taken, in large measure, by the state. In the government's own words:[19]

> Democratic planning involves the acceptance by the people of the Plans and the sacrifices associated with them. The market mechanism is retained; so also the parliamentary institutions, the free press, the free trade union movement and the other freedoms that go with democracy.
>
> Democratic values can be fostered only in conditions in which the citizens have a fair opportunity of work and a reasonable standard of living. The Plans thus stress the economic objectives of raising the national income and living standards.
>
> ... The state has to initiate development on a broad front. It must plan its own investment and influence and regulate economic activity within the private sector so as to ensure the co-ordinated development of all the available resources.

The major objectives of the First Five-Year Plan (1951-6) were: to arrest the rise in prices which had resulted from wartime inflation; to try to make good the shortage of raw materials and essential consumer goods; to help to rehabilitate the millions of refugees displaced by Partition. The long-term objective was to start a process of planned growth. To this end the government set aside 24 billion rupees,[20] while the private sector invested an estimated 16 billion rupees. The increase in the national income which was expected to result from these public and private investments combined was calculated at 11 per cent. Investment was expected to go up from an annual rate of $4\frac{1}{2}$ billion rupees in the first year of the plan to $6\frac{3}{4}$ billion rupees in the fifth year, or from 5 to 7 per cent of the national income. The planners allocated government's resources as follows: 15 per cent on agriculture; 30 per cent on irrigation and power; 5 per cent on industry and mining; 26 per cent on transport and communications; 21 per cent on social services. As can be seen from these percentages, the main priorities of the plan were agricul/ture and the rehabilitation of the transport system which had been run down during the war.

As far as agriculture was concerned most of the government's efforts went on decreasing the cultivator's dependence on the mon/soon by spreading irrigation. For this there were obvious reasons. The cultivator had to be given an assured source of water if India's dependence on the outside world for her food was to be reduced. Irrigation has always been a traditional governmental activity, from the days of Mohenjodaro through the days of British rule and it so happened that there were a large number of government irrigation schemes ready by 1947; work was going on on some of them at the time of the transfer of power.

The priority given to agriculture and the railways was sensible. But in 1951 India was still new to planning. The First Five/Year Plan was a list of projects rather than a careful calculation of balances between one sector of the economy and another. No real decisions were taken as to what sort of plan India should have, no start was made on increasing steel production for which India is exceptionally well endowed. Instead, many major multi/purpose irri/gation/cum/power generation schemes were started simultaneously. This was putting the emphasis in the wrong place for an economy already suffering from inflation, since these schemes have a long period of gestation. It would have been better to have less major dams and more tube wells and pond clearing.

Until 1951 only 17 per cent of India's usable water was used for irrigation; the rest ran waste to the sea. By the end of the Second Five/Year Plan, water utilization had gone up by 10 per cent and it is expected that it will have gone up by another 10 per cent at the end of the Third Five/Year Plan. The increase in irrigation has been achieved in two ways. A great deal of water utilization is created by minor projects which range from sinking tube wells, diesel wells and ordinary village wells, to building weirs, small dams, storage reservoirs and digging or dredging tanks (ponds), the traditional south Indian way of storing water. Roughly half the additional irrigation has been achieved through such minor schemes scattered over the whole of India. The other half has been added by the major schemes, which have taken anything up to 15 years to complete. Because of the political need to satisfy every region that it is not being forgotten, these major schemes have been distributed across India in such a way that nearly all the major rivers have been taken in hand.

In northern India, the Bhakra Dam, the highest gravity dam in the world, has been built at a cost of £130 million to irrigate over $3\frac{1}{2}$ million acres of land in the Punjab and Rajasthan and to generate 600,000 Kw of electricity. In Orissa, the longest dam in the world, the Hirakud, has been completed at a cost of £50 million; it provides water for nearly four million acres of land and generates 123,000 Kw of electric power. In eastern India, the Damodar Valley Corporation, patterned upon the Tennessee Valley Authority, has been set up to protect large tracts of land in Bihar and Bengal from floods and erosion, and to provide, from its own four dams and three thermal power stations, over $1\frac{1}{2}$ million Kw of electric power to serve the Ruhr of India. In southern India, the Tungabhadra Dam has been erected to irrigate 830,000 acres of land in Andhra and Mysore; it will, however, produce little electricity. Between them, the big and the small irrigation projects have been adding each year about half a million acres to the amount already under irrigation and since 1961 the increase has been of the order of 700,000 acres a year; it is expected that by the end of the Third Five-Year Plan the annual increase will have gone up to 900,000 acres. But as is always the case with irrigation there tends to be a time-lag between the utilization of the water and its supply.

Electric power is spreading even faster than irrigation, not only from the high dams of the great multi-purpose schemes, but also from special schemes to generate electricity either through diesel or thermal stations – as in Bokaro – or nuclear power stations or specially constructed dams like the Koyna Dam in Maharashtra. Every year great effort is put into generating more electric power because India's need for electricity is endless and there is a terrible shortage of it. Without electricity, in a country with little oil and whose coal is mostly tucked away in one corner, neither heavy industry nor small scale industry can develop. The development of electric power is a continuous

184

process. In the First Five-Year Plan the available amount of electric power was brought up from 2,300,000 Kw to 3,400,000 Kw. This was 200,000 Kw less than the planned target because of difficulty in getting the machinery required from abroad, especially transmission equipment. In the Second Five-Year Plan, as we shall see, more effort went into generating electricity in an attempt to catch up.

During the war the transport system in India, as everywhere else, had been run down and great efforts were made in the First Five-Year Plan to bring the railways back to their old efficiency, at a cost of £315 million.[21] The extra traffic carried paid a return on rehabilitation and left a profit for further expansion in the bargain. The Indian railways are one of the very few left in the world that pay.

As well as the railways, the government concentrated upon the roads. There was a programme for national highways – which continues to be given a high priority particularly along the border areas now that conflict with China makes the policing of the Himalayas vital. In addition to national highways there were state highways and finally, right at the bottom of the scale, the village roads. Much had to be done, indeed, much still remains to be done. India does not have enough roads; the roads there are are not wide enough, not enough of them are properly surfaced and few of them are properly bridged. In 1951 only a few roads were properly surfaced while on many major roads, the Bombay–Delhi road, for instance, lack of bridges over the major rivers interrupted traffic for days on end during the monsoon. The road expansion programme is bound to take a long time. Some of the rivers to be bridged are miles wide, others are almost unpredictable, being miles wide during the rains and a mere trickle in between. Others, rivers like the Kosi, keep changing their bed with a peripatetician's lack of discrimination, creating havoc as they move. The main highways are only one of the aspects of the transport rehabilitation programme; just as important are the village approach roads. Most Indian villages are cut off from market because they have no approach road, only parallel cart ruts through the fields which turn into torrents of mud

185

during the monsoon, and are ruinously bumpy for lorries in the dry weather. Yet, if agriculture is to become an industry like any other, it is essential that goods should be easily transportable to market, and this means more village approach roads.[22]

By and large, the First Five/Year Plan was an agricultural plan. Nearly half of the government's expenditure over the five years was spent directly or indirectly upon agriculture. Community projects, irrigation, multi/purpose projects and the like took the bulk. A quarter of the remaining expenditure was spent on transport, and one/fifth on education, health, housing, welfare, refugee rehabilitation and other such items.

The aim of the plan had been modest: to increase the national income by 11 per cent so that there should be something left over after the 1·3 per cent calculated increase in population; to give people hope of a better future for their children. The results exceeded the hopes of the planners. The national income went up by 18·5 per cent over the five years; agricultural production rose by 22 per cent, industrial production by 39 per cent, production of capital goods by 70 per cent and that of intermediate goods and consumer goods by 34 per cent.

Indians learn from experience more than most people. After 1947 they had rapidly resigned themselves to the discovery that the rivers did not flow with milk and honey just because Independence had come. Now, in the middle 1950s they became plan minded. Had the First Five/Year Plan been a failure, planning would have been given up without hesitation. But since planning had succeeded so spectacularly, it became the Sesame of everybody's aspirations overnight.

The First Five/Year Plan was surrounded by three very favour/able circumstances. First, the weather was kind. With the exception of a famine localized to Bihar, which was averted by the timely gift/cum/loan of two million tons of American wheat, and a prolonged drought in five districts in Madras, there were bumper crops almost everywhere. Secondly, the Korean war created a price boom for India's exports. Finally, India was not short of foreign exchange with which to pay for imports of machinery, raw materials

186

and food. India had no difficulty in paying for the equipment required for the plan, and private entrepreneurs had no difficulty in obtaining import licences for the machinery they needed to rehabilitate and expand their plants, or to start new ones.

Unfortunately for India, by the time the Second Five-Year Plan was launched in 1956, the same favourable circumstances no longer operated. The Korean war was over, the boom it had created was over, the weather began to be unkind. Fortunately, India had as a cushion its wartime accumulation of sterling balances. These sterling balances had been earned by India at the cost of great sacrifices during the war and British politicians felt honour-bound to let India draw upon sterling as much as she wanted, regardless of the consequences to Britain. Well before the end of the Second Five-Year Plan these sterling balances had been reduced to a minimum below which it would be dangerous to go, but meanwhile they had performed their invaluable function of permitting Indian growth to continue without interruption in the years before the democratic world as a whole realized that it had a vested interest in India's success. Once the balances had been used up, India had to depend upon her exports, which it will be remembered are not elastic, and upon aid, to fill its gap in foreign exchange; a gap which turned out to be much larger than had been anticipated at the time when the Second Five-Year Plan was drafted.

The Second Five-Year Plan was more sophisticated than the first. The government had taken heart from the success of the first plan, and set about to spend twice as much on the second plan as it had spent on the first. Much of the extra expenditure was earmarked for heavy industry, notably steel, and the transport, electricity, iron ore and limestone required for a five-fold expansion of steel production. This time the planners set out not only to raise the national income sufficiently to provide for a further rise in the standard of living but also to create enough jobs to provide for those coming onto the labour market. It was calculated that 10 million more people would have to be employed in 1961 than in 1956, and to reduce inequalities in income and wealth. Forty-eight billion rupees were earmarked for the public sector, 38 billion of which were to be invested; the rest was needed for such services as education and health. In addition the private sector was supposed to invest 24 billion rupees. Thus the rate of investment was expected to go up from 7 per cent of the national income in the first year of the plan to 11 per cent in the last year. This in turn was expected to produce a growth in the national income of nearly 5 per cent per year, against the first plan's 3·5 per cent.

The government announced what it would allow the private sector to undertake and what it reserved for itself. With the exception of oil and coal mining, the division was not doctrinaire. The key decision to put three steel plants in the public sector was as much the consequence of the failure of private enterprise to find the money as of any devotion to socialism. It was felt that if the government had to do most of the financing it might as well run the projects. The planners allocated 11·8 per cent of the outlay in the public sector to agriculture, 19 per cent to irrigation and power, 18·6 per cent to industry and mining, 28·9 per cent to transport and communica, tions, 21·7 per cent to the social services. And they proposed to finance the public sector from an additional 4·5 billion rupees of extra taxation, 7 billion rupees of public loans, 5 billion rupees of small savings, 1·5 billion rupees from the earnings of the rail, ways, 2·5 billion rupees from the unfunded debt and miscellaneous capital receipts, 8 billion rupees of foreign aid, 12 billion rupees of deficit financing, and 4 billion rupees to be raised by additional measures.

The core of the Second Five-Year Plan was steel. Three government steel plants for about one million tons of steel each, were to be completed; one at Bhilai, with Soviet assistance, one at Rourkela with German assistance, one at Durgapur with British assistance. In addition the two steel mills in the private sector, at Jamshedpur and Burnpur, were to be doubled in the plan period.

The decision to concentrate on steel was sensible. On the one hand, India has been importing a lot of steel and will need more and more as she develops. On the other hand India has some of the world's largest deposits of high-grade iron ore located not far from coal and water, and a very cheap labour force together with a

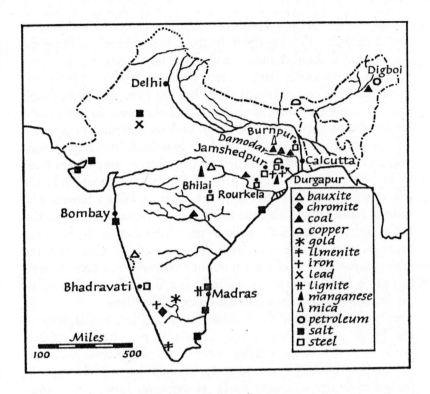

Map showing mineral resources

considerable skilled middle class from which to develop the necessary technicians. Except for Australia, India can produce the cheapest steel in the world. Already it had in Jamshedpur the biggest steel mill in the Commonwealth and at the beginning of the Second Five-Year Plan India was producing 1·3 million tons of steel a year. By the end of the plan it had hoped to produce six million tons a year, while coal output would go up from 38 to 60 million tons a year. To meet the demand of the new steel mills and the expansion of the existing ones, new railway lines were programmed, and there was also to be a large increase in electric generation from 3·4 to 6·9 million Kw, partly for steel, partly for more general industrial and agricultural uses.

189

Early in the Second Five-Year Plan, India ran into difficulties and there was a slowing down in the rate of expansion. From the beginning the weather turned unfavourable. During the first three years an unexpectedly large amount of cereals had to be imported. In addition the cost of capital goods imports rose, and it was found that the import content of the plan and the need for spares and imported raw materials had been underestimated. As a result foreign exchange reserves dropped by two-thirds and import controls had to be severely tightened while assistance was sought from all friendly countries to fill the gap in foreign exchange which by the end of the second plan had grown to over 21 billion rupees. The World Bank created an Aid-India Club comprising most of the major industrial countries of the West, which met for the first time in 1958. Neither the very large assistance of the Club nor the relatively modest aid of the communist countries has been enough to enable India to ease her controls, but it has been adequate to prevent any really serious slowing down of the plan.

Over the five years of the Second Five-Year Plan, in fact, income rose by 20 per cent against the planned 25 per cent; agricultural production, despite the weather, went up by 20 per cent. Industrial production, although considerably affected by the shortfall in foreign exchange still went up by 41 per cent. Indeed, it is noteworthy that while investment in the public sector fell seriously short of the planned amount, investment in the private sector exceeded expectations, and by the end of the second plan, private investment for both plans put together exceeded targets by 11 billion rupees. During the second plan the rate of investment had increased from 8 per cent of the national income at the beginning of the plan to some 11 per cent at the end. Government revenue went up by three-quarters as a result of drastic increases in taxation, especially indirect taxation, the actual increase in taxation for the five years being 10·5 billion rupees. Taking both plans together agricultural production went up by 46 per cent, industrial production by 95 per cent, national income by 43 per cent, per capita income by some 18 per cent. There was enough on the credit side to encourage the planners into sufficient optimism to draw up a Third Five-Year

Plan rather over half as large again as the second, in the hope that this would help the Indian economy to take off into what the economists call self-sustaining growth.

The Third Five-Year Plan (1961–6), aims at raising the national income by over 5 per cent per year. The planners provided for an outlay of 75 billion rupees in the public sector and 41 billion rupees in the private sector. Of the outlay in the public sector 10·6 billion rupees is earmarked for agriculture, 6·5 billion rupees for irrigation, 10 billion for power, 14 billion for industry and mining, 14·8 billion for transport and communications, 13 billion for social services. The public sector was to be financed in the following way: existing taxes 5·5 billion rupees, railway receipts 1 billion rupees, surplus of other public enterprises 4·5 billion rupees, additional taxation 17 billion rupees, public loan 8 billion rupees, small savings 6 billion rupees, provident funds 2·6 billion rupees, steel equalization fund 1 billion rupees, miscellaneous capital receipts 1·7 billion rupees, deficit financing 5·5 billion rupees, foreign assistance 22 billion rupees. The foreign exchange gap was estimated at 33·6 billion rupees. The rate of investment is expected to go up from 11 to 14 per cent of the national income by the last year.

The Third Five-Year Plan was even better balanced than the second. It aimed at increasing food grains production from 79 to 100 million tons over the five years; the area under irrigation from 70 to 90 million acres; electricity from 5·6 to 12·7 million Kw; coal extraction from 55 to 97 million tons; iron ore extraction from 10·8 to 30 million tons; finished steel capacity from 4·5 to 7·5 million tons.

Unfortunately the third plan ran into difficulties from the very start. On the one hand there were shortfalls carried over from the second into the third plan; particularly serious bottlenecks which still had to be cleared, for instance steel production at the beginning of the third plan was only half of the installed capacity and there had been grave transport bottlenecks due to shortages of coal and waggons which had in turn affected steel production and the generation of thermal power. On the other hand, the census results gave a jolt to the planners who had assumed a population increase of 2 per cent per annum; the census figures indicate that the annual increase is nearer 2·8 per cent. Also, the Chinese aggression in the autumn of 1962 affected the plan drastically. The armed forces had gone up to 900,000 and defence expenditure by 1964 had trebled from what it had been at the beginning of the third plan. And to make the outlook bleaker, in the United States there will be severe cuts in the Foreign Aid Programme upon which India depends to carry out her plan. As a result there has been pressure to trim the plan; to cut out the inessentials and to concentrate to a greater extent upon agriculture and activities like the production of fertilizer which will reduce the import bill.

To sum up the plans so far. What are the achievements, and what are the difficulties?

The achievements are considerable. Food production has gone up; India has the makings of an industrial base as the core of the plan keeps expanding. By and large the right priorities have been applied and the bottlenecks do get tackled in time. But what is most impressive is the willingness with which the Indian citizen, whether he is a university graduate or an illiterate peasant, is prepared to stake his country's future on the plans. Taxation has shot up in India in a way it has never done in any democratic country except in times of war, and yet the people go on voting for the plans with even greater zest than they vote for the Congress Party. Such determination and willingness to go without today in order that one's grandchildren may not go short, deserves reward indeed.

Another very hopeful sign that India is developing in the right direction is the extraordinary vigour of the private sector; more particularly the medium-scale industries have taken advantage of the plans to spring up everywhere where there is power and raw materials available to them. There has been an entrepreneurial explosion all over Indian cities and industrial estates. India now manufactures almost everything from transistor radios – in the public sector – to sewing machines – in the private sector – which sell in Britain and Australia in competition with old established makes. Those are two examples, but every year India manufactures something that previously had to be imported. There is no doubt that of all the developing countries India is the one which has the will and the middle class required for development of a self-sustaining kind. However, development is not yet within reach; the difficulties are still formidable.

First, the failures of the plans show that it will take a long time before India can be self-sufficient in food, especially if the population goes on increasing at the present rate. Shortage of foreign exchange is the greatest obstacle to development and this shortage is going to get worse, at least till the end of the century when the Ninth Five-Year Plan may at last see India over the hump. Hand in hand with the shortage of foreign exchange there is a shortage of technicians and administrators, not as acute as in some other developing countries, but nevertheless sufficiently acute to have created bottle-necks in the second and third plans. But such shortages can be cured by aid, not just financial aid but technical assistance as well. What cannot be cured so readily, at least for the time being, is the strain put upon India's meagre resources by the threat of her population explosion.

The greatest challenge to India's future comes from the increase in population. During the decade 1911–21 India's population had actually decreased, but ever since then it has been increasing thanks to the steady advance in hygiene, preventive medicine, and communications which make it possible to rush food where it is wanted. The last time there was a famine in which large numbers of people died was 1943 in Bengal. In addition to vaccination, chlorination of wells, and inoculation there has been a breakthrough in chemicals which has greatly reduced the death rate. DDT spraying has reduced the incidence of malaria, which used to kill one million people in India a year, to such an extent that many more people now die from TB, than from malaria. As a result of all these advances, life expectation in India has gone up by 10 years; people live longer – and the infant mortality rate has been reduced with the result that the increase in population is steadily going up. Before the war when the British government noticed this upward trend it was thought to prove a rise in the standard of living, as indeed it would have done had there been more good land left to bring under cultivation. That this was a mistake can be appreciated if one remembers that India's population went up by 12 millions from 1891 to 1921, by 109 millions between 1921 and 1951, and by 81 millions in the ten years between 1951 and 1961 when the population increased by 2·1 per cent. The latest estimates suggest that the population is now increasing by 2·8 per cent per year, which, since one is dealing with compound interest, means that India will have a population of over 625 million by the end of the Fifth Five-Year Plan. The present increase is not greater than it was in Britain a century ago; there has been no increase in fertility in India, only a drop in mortality.

Left to himself the Indian villager would, so every inquiry suggests, want to have three sons and one daughter, after that he would be quite content to limit his family. The need to have sons is real. It is necessary for Hindus to have a son so that their funeral rites can be performed. If there is no living son, adoption is resorted to, but above all the mother needs a living son to whom she can turn in her old age after she becomes a widow. Unless she has a son whose house she can run she becomes destitute and at the mercy of her in-laws. The need to have one living son prompts the villager to say he wants three, as insurance. In the West, too, people had large families so long as epidemics and infant mortality took a high toll. There is always a time lag between a reduction in the number of births and the number of deaths. It is unlikely that Indians would, given the possibility, go in for small families as was the case in Europe between the wars. They love children too much and in a rural setting there is always something for children to do and somewhere to put them, if only minding goats and babies, or collecting firewood. Except for the Roman Catholics and the more orthodox Muslims, nobody in India has any religious objection to birth control. There is no religious taboo, no injunction to multiply, although there is a strong feeling that the woman who bears sons is blessed by the gods, and barrenness is as terrible in the Indian village as it is portrayed in *Yerma*, the play by the famous Spanish author Federico García Lorca. But once there are three or four living sons only ignorance prevents women from using contraceptives; ignorance and the nagging tongue of their mother-in-law who often does not see why her daughter-in-law should not bear a child every year, as she did herself. As the joint family dissolves, as more women become educated they are more and more willing to space and limit their families, once they learn that children though God-given can be planned. The problem of family planning in India is therefore twofold: first, education; next, contraception of a kind which is sufficiently cheap and straightforward to be applied in the conditions of overcrowding and lack of privacy of Indian rural life.

The government of India is fully aware of the need to curb the population explosion. Family planning was included in the Second Five-Year Plan. At the beginning of the plan there were already 147 clinics in operation; at the end of the plan there were 1,649, which is a thousand clinics short of what had been planned. The shortage was due to the shortage in trained staff, rather than shortage in demand. In the Third Five-Year Plan £21 million have been allocated to family planning over the five years; and there is a provision to spend up to £37½ million if need be. The problem is not to find the money so much as to find a method which will meet India's needs. There are not enough doctors or mobile vans. Most of the clinics are in urban areas and the villages have hardly been touched with the exception of Madras state and parts of Maharashtra where almost half a million men have submitted to voluntary vastectomy in order to limit their families. However, male sterilization is only a stop-gap measure until the day when a pill which has to be taken orally only once a month has been discovered. The urgency of the problem is best shown by the fact[23] that the government of India has the choice between spending £45 on providing each new baby with health, education and capital investment if it is not to grow up to add to the millions of unemployed, or spending £45 on preventing its birth. That there is no time to lose is obvious. After all, the labour force of 1991 will have been born by 1971, only one and a half plans away. Unless India grows 120 million tons of cereals by 1970, her people will be eating less than they do today if the outside world does not fill a food-gap which could well be of the order of 30 million tons.

86 Pandit Jawaharlal Nehru, India's first Prime Minister, was admired and loved by all India's people. At his funeral procession thousands lined the route.

87 One of the aims of the five-year plans instituted by Nehru in the 1950s was the utilization of water. The newly completed Bhakra Dam in the Punjab irrigates 3½ million acres of land.

88 The Hirakud Dam in Orissa is the longest in the world.

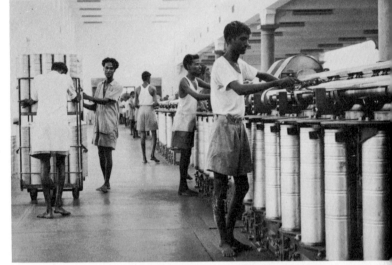

89 (*above*) The production of refined petroleum products began in the 1960s. This is one of India's four large oil refineries at Trombay.

90 (*centre*) This textile mill at Madura illustrates the use of modern equipment.

91 The core of the Second Five-Year Plan (1956–61) was steel. This wheel is being tested at the Durgapur steelworks in West Bengal which was completed with British assistance.

92 Gandhi aimed at making women active participants in the building of the Indian nation. These women are testing telephones at a factory in Bangalore.

93 At a factory in Mysore.

94 There is a great shortage of nurses in India and education has helped to overcome this problem.

95 Social education centres such as this one have been established in the villages.

96 The relationship between India and China was one of peaceful co-existence until 1962. Nehru on a visit to Peking (Premier Chou En-Lai, centre).

97 In autumn 1962 China attacked India. These tribesmen, preparing for a war-dance, come from the part of the NEFA claimed by China.

98 Tibet, which had been independent for forty years, was attacked by China in 1950. These Tibetan refugees were among the many who fled to India.

99 Lal Bahadur Shastri, India's Prime Minister, has the twofold problem of solving India's internal difficulties and her external tension with China. At a Hindu ceremony.

स्वास्थ्य और सुख-चैन के लिए

परिवार नियोजन

100 The most important challenge to India's future lies in her increase in population.
A new family planning centre at New Delhi.

11   Foreign Policy

INDIA IS NEWLY INDEPENDENT, non-white – poor. These facts provide the background to her foreign policy.

Like most ex-colonies India began in 1947 with a way of looking at the world different from that of the Western democracies. Most educated Indians had a certain bias against the West and for the communist countries. Indians believed the communists had no colour prejudice and no colonies. They remembered very clearly that westerners had. Colour prejudice had been shown against them in their own country, and in 1947 the world was still full of Western colonies. Moreover, India wanted to draw her policy on a clean slate uncluttered by past alliances or ties. This slate was, however, not as clean as Indians thought, for all their ideas were influenced by their experience of the Pax Britannica. They had as a result a somewhat unrealistic view of the world. They took the view that all quarrels could be peacefully settled, partly because for a century and a half an attack on India would have been an attack on Britain. With the exception of the short-lived scare of the Second World War, when the Japanese threw a few bombs on Indian cities and advanced to the borders of Assam, there had been no attack on India and India had been lulled into regarding the Himalayas as insuperable and her Asian neighbours as necessarily friendly. Events have shown how wrong both assumptions were.

Like most of the ex-colonies which have become independent after India, she was unwilling to take sides in the cold war. They recognized that the Soviet Union was a dictatorship but they thought the Western powers were imperialist. They mostly recognized that Russia had no political democracy but they were inclined to suspect that the Western powers had no economic democracy. Seen from Delhi, the cold war looked like a quarrel in which many Indians wished to take no side. They saw it not in black and white but in shades of grey. They were too absorbed in their own problems to bother about what happened to Western Europe so long as it did not affect them. Moreover, they felt they were too poor and too weak to be able to contribute anything militarily useful.

This at least was the set of attitudes which lay behind Nehru's enunciation of the policy of nonalignment. This policy, which for several years caused great irritation in the West, particularly in the United States, was challenged by hardly anybody in India, nor was it abandoned on Nehru's death. There were several reasons why it was accepted so readily. The Congress Party had always left foreign affairs to Nehru; most senior Congressmen had never been abroad and took his word on foreign affairs. The communists who would have liked to take India into the Soviet orbit dared not say so. The rightists who wanted to take India into the American orbit dared not say so either. A compromise on nonalignment suited everybody, especially since nonalignment fits very well into the Hindu way of looking at things – a way which is so good at spotting every conceivable nuance of grey.

Through the 1950s the Indian attitude did not change. Indians discovered more and more about the weaknesses of the Soviet system, they could not ignore the Soviet suppression of the Hungarian revolution or Khrushchev's condemnation of Stalin. On the other hand they argued that the American support for Franco, Chiang KaiShek and Bao Dai showed that the West talks democracy when it suits it but also backs dictators when it suits it. This feeling was of course exacerbated by American military aid to Pakistan and by the military pacts of SEATO and CENTO, which – as distinct from NATO – seemed to them to add nothing to the balance of power and invited aggression; and aggression in Asia.

Indians were gradually disillusioned about the Soviet Union which they came to see as just another great power rather than as the struggling developing country which had built itself from almost nothing – Nehru's original picture.

The new hero of the 1950s was China. The slogan was 'Hindi, Chini, Bhai, Bhai!' – Chinese and Indians are brothers! The talk was of 2,000 years of peace and of how the Chinese communists were making China great again. There were some, nevertheless, who wondered how a great China would be in India's interest, but their doubts were firmly muted by Nehru's insistence on the Five Prin-ciples of Co-existence to which China subscribed – so he thought.

The principles were unexceptionable; indeed, they have been practised by all nations in times of peace and were not worth formulating. They are: Respect for each other's territorial integrity and sovereignty; Non-aggression; Non-interference in each other's internal affairs; Equality and mutual benefit; and peaceful co-existence. Unfortunately, as India was to discover, good intentions are no substitute for deterrent force.

In the first years of independence Pakistan and Britain filled the Indian horizon.

Relations with Pakistan were bound to be bad to start with, for Pakistan had come about as the result of a proper civil war and there were many people who felt real grievances just as there were many disputes which had not been solved at the time of the transfer of power. The fault for the perpetual tension between India and Pakistan goes to both sides, though Indians would argue that Pakistan has been more aggressive towards India than India towards Pakistan. This can probably be substantiated by a detailed study of all the crises which have kept relations festering, but fails to take into account the frustration of Pakistan at being so much India's smaller brother. The tension between the two countries has oscillated like a temperature chart; there was a peak in 1950 when millions of Hindus from East Pakistan ran to India for safety. There has been another peak every time the Kashmir question crops up at the UN. The highest tension, however, was reached when Pakistan tried to prevent India from obtaining military aid against the Chinese attack in 1962 on the ground that the arms would be used against Pakistan and that India had entered into a conspiracy with China to get arms for herself. The tension between the two countries has been kept alive by the treatment of minorities in Pakistan, by the dispute over canal waters – now settled thanks to the World Bank – by border shootings, by boundary claims – settled through negotiations after much bickering – by a constant arms race, by the Kashmir question, and in spring 1965 by the dispute over the boundary in the Rann of Kutch.

So long as relations remain tense between India and Pakistan neither country can effectively protect its northern frontier for there can be no joint defence policy and most of the armed forces are frozen in front of each other instead of policing the real danger spots on the Himalayas. The latest example of the stupidity to which IndoPakistan relations can lead was the desire of India for submarines to match those Pakistan was going to get from the United States. This was at a time when what India needed was to be able to defend her border with China, and to protect her neighbours Nepal, Bhutan and Sikkim from becoming Chinese satellites. A look at the map should suffice to convince Indians that submarines are not what they need, specially as there is little evidence to suggest that China is a naval power.

One of the very first decisions India had to take on becoming independent was to settle her relations with Britain. Britain had for a century and a half been India's window on the world, so she quite naturally loomed larger in Indian eyes in 1947 than either Russia or America. The first issue was whether a Republic could stay in the Commonwealth.

The ties between the two countries were real despite the long struggle, perhaps indeed because of the long struggle and the way in which both sides had, thanks to Mahatma Gandhi, refrained from an escalation into terrorism. The credit, one cannot repeat it often enough, for this adherence to peaceful methods, goes to the Mahatma. Had Indians resorted to terrorism, the British would most probably have resorted to counterterrorism. As far back as 1929, at the Lahore Session of the Congress Party, Nehru had stated that:

If we use the word independence we do so in no sense hostile to the larger ideal. Independence for us means complete freedom from British domination and British imperialism. Having attained our freedom I have no doubt that India will welcome all attempts at world co-operation and federation, and will even agree to give up a part of her own independence to a larger group of which she is an equal member.

India stayed in the Commonwealth without any surrender of sovereignty as Nehru was to point out in Parliament when he answered communist criticisms. The relationship was wholly to India's advantage, entailing no liability for India, putting duties upon Britain as became obvious when the British tried to get into the Common Market in 1962.

However, the links between India and Britain are not wholly selfish and go far beyond any formal relationship as Sardar Panikkar, the Indian historian, explained:

It is not correct to say that the likemindedness which exists today between India and England is a superficial one. It is based on a common experience of 150 years of history. The inheritance from Britain is of even greater importance than the Hindu tradition of the past. Modern India does not live under the laws of Manu. Its mental background and equipment have been moulded into their present shape by over a hundred years of Western education extending over every aspect of mental activity. Its social ideas are derived predominantly from the liberalism of the nineteenth century. Therefore this likemindedness is a major fact. . . . India's close association with a world-wide group of nations gives her a prestige and influence which she would not otherwise possess. The Commonwealth today is a major political factor in Asia. Its importance will increase in proportion to the degrees of co-operation between Britain and India. The Common-wealth has therefore come to mean something for India.[24]

As Sardar Panikkar makes clear, for India the Commonwealth is Britain, and the Commonwealth suits India because it adds to her stature. These are the twin reasons for which the Republic of India stayed in the Commonwealth.

209

Next to the Commonwealth, India takes an interest in the UNO as is shown by her repeated willingness to provide one ambulance or troops or a General for those of the UN's policing actions of which she approves, from Korea and the Gaza strip to the Congo and Cyprus. Within the UN India was the original creator of the Afro-Asian bloc. It was Nehru, too, who convened an Asian Conference in 1949 to consider the problems of Indonesian independence. In 1954 it was India which took the lead in helping to secure a truce in Indo-China; it was India which brought China into the comity of the Afro-Asians at Bandung in 1955 and repeatedly urged the right of the Chinese communists to the Chinese seat at the UN.

Nehru's foreign policy has been of great help to the West. He warned constantly – in good English – that the sands of imperialism were running out. All colonial powers, with the exception of Portugal, have listened to him to their own advantage. But telling the West what to do was of singularly little use to India herself. India's own immediate interests were not in Algeria or the Congo but on her borders, yet Nehru took so global a view that he neglected India's borders. Relations with Pakistan have become worse over the years, very largely because of Nehru's incapacity to negotiate a compromise, so that India was left with an enemy on her longest and most vulnerable frontier. Relations with Burma have never been more than formal despite the fact that part of India's defences lie in Burma and that there were many Indian settlers in Burma. Indeed many Indians were expelled from Burma in 1964. Relations with Ceylon have never been really cordial, and India failed to get proper treatment for the Indians who were sent to Ceylon's tea gardens as indentured labourers. However, an agreement on the fate of these Indians was reached after Nehru's death. Relations with Nepal are bedevilled by suspicion and fear of the big brother. Nehru mishandled the Goan situation from the beginning and discredited himself by the manner in which he occupied the Portuguese enclave in contravention to the method of peaceful negotiation he had been preaching to the rest of the world. The most serious mistake in Nehru's conduct of India's foreign policy was his obsession with Pakistan; an obsession which made him overlook China. As a result India was both unprepared and without allies when China attacked in the autumn of 1962. Obsession with Pakistan and Kashmir have had another effect upon the way Nehru interpreted non-alignment. Because he needed a Russian veto on Kashmir at the Security Council he became neutral on the side of the Iron Curtain. He only spoke up against Russia's action in Hungary when he was forced to by the pressure of his own public opinion, and he gave the very vocally anti-American Krishna Menon *carte blanche* at the UN for years. This was at great expense not only to Indo-American relations but to Indo-African relations, for Krishna Menon somehow managed to make many African delegates feel like 'black monkeys' as one of them complained privately.

In the case of Tibet Nehru allowed expediency to override prudence and morality. Tibet, India's natural buffer with China, had been independent for 40 years when the Chinese invaded in 1950. Instead of proclaiming this as the imperialism it was – nobody expected India to do more than that – Nehru supported Peking on the ground that Tibet was a Province of China. His reward was China's encroachments in Ladakh and the claims on the North East Frontier Agency. But only in 1962 when the Chinese attacked India did Nehru admit that he had been living in 'a fool's paradise'. However, short of a renewed Chinese attack it is unlikely that India will give up non-alignment, although she may be pushed into the manufacture of nuclear arms by relentless Chinese provocation rather than accept the Western offer of a 'nuclear umbrella'. What Lal Bahadur Shastri would like is a multilateral declaration by the great powers that they will keep Asia free from nuclear aggression. Western support in 1962 was much more immediate and extensive than Russia's, but it was clear that Russia disapproved of the Chinese attack, and India does not want either to add Russia to her enemies or to lose the Russian veto in her favour over Kashmir at the UN. Moreover, nobody in the West is now pressing India to become an ally. The Americans no longer want bases in India, and India's Western friends, however willing they may be to defend India should it become necessary, do not want to have to fight a war with China over Aksaichin.

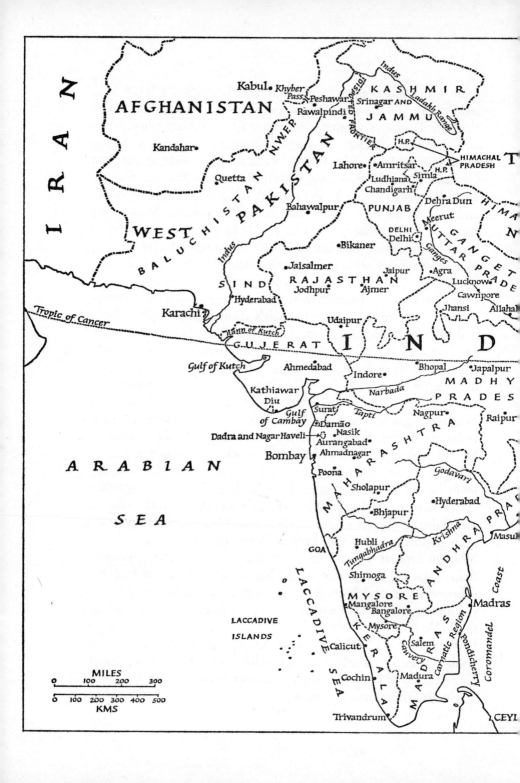

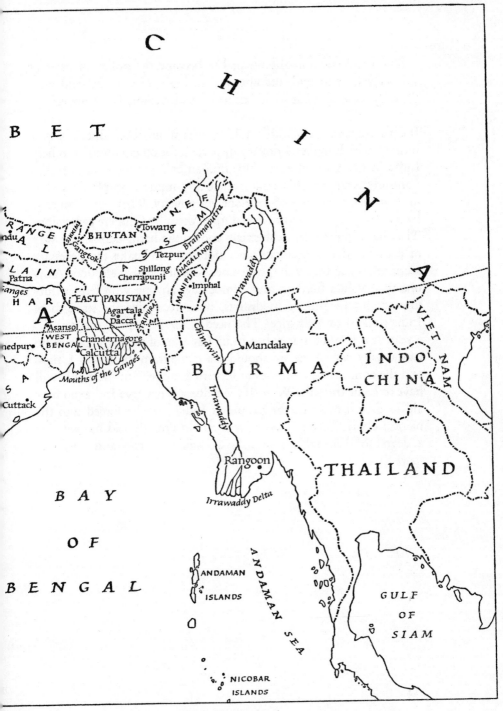

Political map of India

The policy of non-alignment has become the policy of most of Afro-Asia, often with the approval of both sides in the cold war; the only country it has so far harmed is its inventor, India herself.

India's trustfulness towards China was a mistake. But it was a mistake which makes it doubly important for other countries to help India in her hour of need. One human being in six lives in India. Painfully, with much sacrifice, these 475 million people are trying to drag themselves out of their ancient poverty. They are hampered by the defence expenditure forced upon them by Chinese aggression. They have, moreover, deliberately chosen the hard, democratic way of consent. If the electorate does not want to make the necessary sacrifices, it can throw the government out at the next election. Anyone who values freedom and democracy, anyone who feels a duty towards his neighbour in distress, must recognize the strength of India's claim to assistance. The need is for perhaps £500 million a year. It is a lot of money but India has a lot of people. There is no reason why part of the aid should not come from the Soviet Union and the communist countries of Eastern Europe. But most of it will have to come from the West. If the affluent states give India too little aid or give it too late, the people of India may be forced into the painful choice between too slow a rate of growth and too extreme a degree of belt-tightening. It is a choice we can and ought to spare them.

Notes on the text

1 The blueprint was extremely complicated; it involved a number of steps including a plebiscite for the NWFP.

2 Assamese, Bengali, Gujerati, Hindi, Kannada, Kashmiri, Malayalam, Marathi, Oriya, Punjabi, Sanskrit, Tamil, Telugu and Urdu. Sub-sequently English was given the status of an associate language.

3 Seven per cent increase instead of an 11 per cent target per year in the Third Five-Year Plan; it is estimated that by 1970 India will require 120 million tons of food grains. However, in 1964–5 the total production was only of the order of 85 million tons.

4 By 1964, after various boundary changes, the Federation consisted of 16 states and 10 small areas under Central administration. The states are: Andhra, Assam, Bihar, Gujerat, Jammu and Kashmir, Kerala, Madhya Pradesh, Madras, Maharashtra, Mysore, Nagaland, Orissa, Punjab, Rajasthan, Uttar Pradesh and West Bengal. The centrally administered areas are: Delhi, Himachal Pradesh, Manipur, Tripura, the Andaman and Nicobar islands; the Laccadive, Minicoy and Amindivi islands; North East Frontier Agency, Dadra and Nagar Haveli; Goa, Daman (ex-Damão) and Diu; Pondicherry.

5 For ten months in the Punjab in 1951–2; for the year in Pepsu in 1953–4; for four months in Andhra in 1954; for 11 months in Travancore-Cochin in 1956–7; and for six months in Kerala in 1959–60.

6 Before 1958 the rupee was divided into 16 annas.

7 To provide education for people from the rural areas is essential. The

number of primary and secondary school children has doubled during the decade 1951–61 and trebled in the case of university students.

8   Junior technical schools further provide training at the secondary level for 10,000 pupils.

9   A caste mostly of better-off farmers who are traditionally anti-Congress. In 1962 the communists got 51 seats out of Andhra's 300; Congress got 176.

10   In 1962 they got 50 seats out of 252 and Congress got 157.

11   Khidwai, Nehru's lieutenant, left the socialists to rejoin the Congress Party in 1952; and Ashok Mehta accepted the Chairmanship of the Planning Commission in 1963.

12   Like Jaya Prakash Narayan, Gandhi's moral heir, who gave up politics in 1955 to devote his life to constructive village work and Vinoba Bhave's Bhoodan Movement.

13   See W.H. Morris-Jones, *The Government and Politics of India*, London 1964, pp. 163–4.

14   The DMK stands for southern regionalism against 'Aryan' supremacy and the exploitation of south India by the north. The best example of this is the attempt to make Hindi the national language.

15   Pro-Peking communist 40; Congress 36; Rebel Congress group 23; Socialists 13; Muslim League 6; pro-Moscow communists 3; Swatantra 1; independents 11 (supported by the communists and the Muslim League). 29 of the new communist legislators are in jail for pro-Chinese sabotage intentions.

8   EQUALITY AND SOCIAL CHANGE

16   As a result of the 1962 elections there were one woman Chief Minister – in Uttar Pradesh, India's largest state – 4 women ministers in the Central government, 11 women ministers in the states, a woman Deputy Chairman of the Upper House of Parliament, 51 women in Parliament and 164 women state legislators.

17   The state of Bombay passed an Act in 1949 making excommunication an offence.

9   AGRICULTURE AND POVERTY

18   The equivalent of a male initiation in the West; only practised by the top three castes.

19 See 'India' pocket book of Economic Information 1963. Govt. of India, Ministry of Finance, Dept of Economic Affairs, p. 199.

20 There are 13·3 rupees to the pound and 4·7619 to the American dollar.

21 380 miles of new lines were constructed and 454 miles of new lines were started. 496 locomotives were added as well as 4,000 carriages and 41,000 waggons.

22 In the First Five-Year Plan 746 miles of missing road links were added, 33 major bridges were built and 5,000 miles of existing roads were repaired.

23 See R. Neild, *Population Policy*. A discussion paper for the ODI, December, 1963.

II FOREIGN POLICY

24 See S. Panikkar, *Will India Stay In?* New Commonwealth, 29 April, 1954.

Select Bibliography

FACTUAL

Todd, J., *Annals and Antiquities of Rajasthan*, London, 1920. Vivid, exciting, romantic and scholarly chronicle of the Rajputs.

Thompson, E., and Garratt, G. T., *Rise and Fulfilment of British Rule in India*, London, 1934. Authoritative and documented account of the British period in India.

Spear, P., *India, Pakistan, and the West*, London, 1943. The best short study of the interaction of the Indian subcontinent and the West.

Wint, G., *The British in Asia*, London, 1947. A wide-ranging survey of South Asia's history, present and future, as governed by British rule and the withdrawal of it.

Hart, H. C., *New India's Rivers*, India, 1956. An exciting and most readable story of the great irrigation projects and the men behind them.

Wallbank, T. W., *A Short History of India and Pakistan*, New York, 1958. An excellent short history, well written and up-to-date.

Edwardes, M., *A History of India*, London, 1961. A useful chronology and an excellent selection of quotations about the past.

The Indian Five-Year Plans, New Delhi, Government of India, 1961 onwards. These reports set forth the targets for the Indian Five-Year Plans, and the policies and the resources behind them.

Ward, B., *India and the West*, London, 1961. An impassioned presentation of India's struggle for progress and the place of aid. An admirable analysis of the cold war and its effect on India.

Moon, P., *Divide and Quit*, London, 1962. A brilliant study of the causes of Partition and a vivid description of the chaos of Partition in the state of Bahawalpur by one who was in charge of maintaining law and order.

Nanda, B. R., *The Nehrus*, London, 1962. A brilliant study of the Nehru family and the alienation of the Indian intellectuals from British rule.

Zinkin, T., *Reporting India*, London, 1962. A description of the worst crises which faced India from 1947 to 1960.

IMAGINATIVE

Forster, E.M., *A Passage to India*, London, 1924.

Gandhi, M.K., *My Experiment with Truth*, India, 1927.

Isherwood, C., and Prabhavananda, S. (translators), *The Song of God: The Bhagavad-Gita*, London, 1951.

Jhabvala, R.P., *To Whom She Will*, London, 1953.

Kipling, R., *Kim*, London, 1901.

Madgulkar, V., *The Village had no Walls*, Bombay, 1958.

Narayan, R.K., *Waiting for the Mahatma*, London, 1955.

Narayan, R.K., *The Guide*, London, 1958.

Nehru, J., *The Discovery of India*, Calcutta, 1946.

Rajagopalachari, C. (translator and editor), *The Mahabharata*, Bombay, 1951.

Rajagopalachari, C. (translator and editor), *The Ramayana*, Bombay, 1958.

Tandon, P.L., *Punjabi Century*, London, 1961.

Acknowledgements

From J. Bernier, *Travels in the Mogul Empire*, 1891, by courtesy of the Trustees of the British Museum, 15; from R. O. Cambridge, *Account of the War in India*, 1761, by courtesy of the Trustees of the British Museum, 20, 24; Camera Press Ltd, 4, 46, 47, 54, 82, 86, 96 (Paul Almasy), 79, 83; by courtesy Davy-Ashmore Ltd., 91; by courtesy Government of India Tourist Office, 5, 6, 7, 48, 66, 71, 85, 87, 88; from A. Hamilton, *New Account of the East Indies*, 1727, by courtesy of the Trustees of the British Museum, 23; by courtesy of the India Office Library, 10, 11, 12, 13, 18, 25, 26, 30, 31, 32, 34, 35; Keystone Press Agency, 37, 43, 59, 68, 96, 97; R. Lannoy, 3, 14, 33, 53, 63, 80, 93; from J. Malcolm, *Life of Clive*, 1836, by courtesy of the Trustees of the British Museum, 28; K. Nath, 100; by courtesy of the Press Information Bureau, Government of India, 27, 38, 39, 40, 42, 44, 45, 49, 50, 51, 58, 60, 61, 62, 64, 66, 67, 69, 84, 89, 92, 94, 95, 98, 99; Radio Times Hulton Picture Library, 8, 9, 19, 22, 29, 36, 41; J. Scheerboom (Mavis Ronson), 52, 57, 74, 75, 76, 77, 78, 90; W. Suschitzky, 1, 2, 17, 56, 65, 72, 73, 81; by courtesy of the Tea Board of India, 70; from E. Terry, *Voyage to East India*, 1655, by courtesy of the Trustees of the British Museum, 16; by courtesy of the Trustees of the British Museum, 21.

Who's Who

ABDULLAH, Sheikh, b. 1905. Socialist politician of Kashmir and founder of National Conference. First political agitation 1938. Quit Kashmir Movement 1946. Prime Minister of Kashmir 1947–52. In jail 1952–64 under preventive detention, and again from 1965.

AKBAR (1556–1605). Moghul Emperor. Tried to reconcile Hindus and Muslims. Was first to evolve a rational administrative system for India. Built Fatehpur Sikri.

ALBUQUERQUE, Alphonso d' (1453–1515). Portuguese explorer. Sailed to India round the Cape of Good Hope. Built a Portuguese fort at Cochin.

BHABHA, Dr H.J., b. 1909. Indian scientist; Chairman Atomic Energy Commission of India.

BUDDHA (c. 567–487 B.C.). Prince of Kapilavastu. Renounced the world and after his Enlightenment became known as The Buddha. Preached Hindu Reformation which, as Buddhism, spread from India to most of Southeast Asia, but was eventually superseded in India by Hinduism itself.

CHAGLA, M.C., b. 1900. Muslim Chief Justice of Bombay 1947–58; diplomat from 1958 to 1962; Education Minister 1962.

CHAVAN, Y.B., b. 1913. Defence Minister of India since 1962. 1960–2 Chief Minister of Bombay. Congressman and Radical Humanist.

CHELMSFORD, Frederick John Napier Thesiger. First Viscount. (1868–1933). British Administrator. Viceroy of India 1916–21. Implemented Montagu-Chelmsford Reforms.

CLIVE, Robert (1725-74). Founder of the Empire of British India. Joined East India Company as writer in Madras at 18. Defeated Suraj Ud Dowlah and secured from Moghul Emperor the Diwani of Bengal, Bihar and Orissa for the Company in 1765.

CORNWALLIS, Charles (1738-1805). Served as Major General in American War of Independence, capitulated at Yorktown 1781. Governor-General of India and Commander-in-Chief of Bengal 1786. Defeated Tipu Sultan at Seringapatam. Framed land-revenue code. Viceroy of Ireland 1798-1801. Returned to India in 1805 to replace Wellesley.

CURZON, George Nathaniel, 1st Marquess of (1859-1925). English Statesman. Viceroy of India 1899-1905. Contributed to Indian agriculture, administration, and archaeology. Partitioned Bengal.

DA GAMA, Vasco (c. 1460-1524). Portuguese navigator and discoverer of the sea route to India. Landed at Calicut 1498.

DALHOUSIE, James Andrew Brown Ronway. 1st Marquess and 10th Earl of (1812-60). Governor-General of India 1848. Fought Second Sikh War, annexed Punjab, Oudh and part of Burma. Great administrator.

DANGE, S.A., b. 1899. Founder of the Communist Party of India. Politician and Trade Unionist. Vice-President World Federation of Trade Unions.

DUPLEIX, Joseph François, General (1697-1763). Governor-General of the French Establishments in India. Rival of Clive.

GANDHI, I., Mrs, b. 1917. Daughter of Pandit Jawaharlal Nehru. Congress President 1959-60. Minister for Information and Broadcasting since 1964.

GANDHI, M. K. (1869-1948). Nationalist leader. Went to South Africa 1893 and stayed there till 1914 to fight for fair treatment for Indians. Returned India 1914 and went into opposition to British rule in 1919. Used peaceful non-co-operation to fight for Indian independence. Murdered 1948.

HASTINGS, W. (1732-1818). First Governor-General of British India; accused of peculation, was impeached in 1786, acquitted in 1795. Reformed the administration of the East India Company, defeated the usurper of Mysore.

HAWKINS, William, Captain (dates not known). Landed Surat 1609. Went to Agra, befriended Emperor Jehangir, defeated him in drinking bout and won permission to erect a factory for the East India Company at Surat.

HUSAIN, Zakir, b. 1897. Muslim educationalist. Since 1962 Vice-President of India.

JINNAH, Mohamed Ali (1876–1948). Lawyer, politician, founder of Pakistan. Leader of Hindu-Muslim separatism from 1930.

KAMARAJ, Nadar, b. 1903. Congress politician and party boss. Ex-Chief Minister of Madras. Since 1964 Congress President.

KHAN, Sayyid Ahmed, Sir (1817–98). Muslim administrator and educationalist; founder Muslim College at Aligarh 1877. Father of the concept of Pakistan.

KRIPALANI, Sucheta, Mrs, b. 1903. Leading woman politician, left Congress in 1951 to join the splinter PSP; elected to Parliament in 1952 and 1957 on PSP (Praja Socialist Party) ticket; rejoined Congress 1958. Became General Secretary of the Congress Party. 1963 elected Chief Minister of Uttah Pradesh, India's biggest state. First woman to be elected Chief Minister in India.

KRISHNAMACHARI, T.T., b. 1892. Business man; joined Congress 1942. Minister for Commerce and Industry 1952–6; in addition Minister for Iron and Steel 1955–7. From 1956–8 Minister for Finance. Had to resign after Judicial Enquiry. From 1964 Finance Minister.

MASANI, M.R., b. 1905. Author, lawyer, politician, co-founder of the right-wing Swatantra Party.

MEHTA, A., b. 1911. Social worker; Chairman of the PSP. Vice-Chairman Planning Commission since 1964 when he joined Congress.

MENON, V.K., b. 1897. Lawyer, politician. Settled in London till 1947. Freeman of St Pancras. High Commissioner for India in London 1947–52; leader Indian Delegation at UN 1952–62. Minister without Portfolio 1956–7. Indian Defence Minister 1957–62. Made to resign over Chinese aggression. Controversial figure known for very left views.

MINTO, Gilbert John Murray Elliot, 4th Earl of (1845–1914). Viceroy of India 1905–10. Introduced separate electorates for Muslims, and MorleyMinto Reform.

MONTAGU, Edwin Samuel (1879–1924). British Liberal politician. UnderSecretary for India 1910–14 under Morley and Crewe. Secretary India Office 1917–22. Piloted the Government of India Bill.

NANDA, G. L., b. 1898. Congress TradeUnion leader and politician. Home Minister of India since 1963.

NARAYAN, Jayaprakash, b. 1902. Sarvodaya leader; Gandhi's spiritual heir; exleader of Socialist Party. In 1957 renounced politics to concentrate on constructive work mostly in the villages.

NEHRU, Jawaharlal (1889–1964). Politician and author. Independent India's first Prime Minister 1947–64. First time Congress President in 1929. Promoted Socialism, planning and nonalignment.

NEHRU, Motilal (1861–1931). Indian lawyer and leader of the Swaraj Party. Father of Jawaharlal.

PATEL, Sardar V. (1875–1950). Gandhian politician. India's first Home Minister and Deputy Prime Minister from 1947 to 1950. Integrated the Princely States.

PATIL, S. K., b. 1900. Gandhian politician and party boss. Has held various positions in the Congress and the Central government. Since 1964 Minister for Communications.

PRASAD, Dr Rajendra (1884–1962). Gandhian politician who became India's first President from 1950 to 1962.

RADHAKRISHNAN, Sir Sarvapalli, F.R.S.I., O.M., b. 1888. Philosopher, theologian, diplomat. Upton Lecturer of Comparative Religion at Oxford. Chairman Executive Board, UNESCO; VicePresident of India 1952–62; President since 1962. Author of many books on Indian philosophy.

RAJAGOPALACHARI, C., b. 1878. Gandhian politician. Author. India's first GovernorGeneral, 1948–50. Founder rightwing Swatantra Party 1959.

REDDY, Sanjiva, b. 1913. Gandhian politician; ex-Chief Minister of Andhra; ex-Congress President. Since 1964 Minister for Steel, Mines and Fuel.

ROY, Ram Mohan (1774–1833). Bengali social reformer. Founded the Brahmo Samaj in 1828; opposed suttee and purdah.

SHASTRI, Lal Bahadur, b. 1904. Gandhian politician from UP. Life Member Servants of the People Society. In jail off and on over a period of 7½ years. Active in UP politics; Secretary-General Congress Party in 1947; Minister for Railways 1951–6, resigned because he felt responsible as minister for derailments. From 1958 to 1961 Minister for Commerce and Industry; from 1961 to 1963 Home Minister; resigned 1963 to set example. Since 1964 Prime Minister of India.

SINGH, Sardar Swaran, b. 1907. Indian politician and Central Minister, at present Minister for External Affairs; belongs to the Sikh community.

SUBRAMANIAM, C., b. 1910. Gandhian politician. Ex-Finance Minister for Madras; from 1962–4 Minister Steel, Mines and Fuel; since 1964 Food Minister.

TAGORE, Sir Rabindranath (1861–1941). Bengali poet, author and educationalist. Founder Shantiniketan. Won Nobel Prize for literature in 1913.

Index

Numbers in italics refer to illustrations

Buddha (*See* Who's Who, p. 221), 20-1
Buddhism, Buddhists, 9, 17, 20-1, 23, 134, *2*
Burkha, 9
Burma, 20, 73; wars in, 39; relations with India, 210
Burnpur, 188
Buxar, battle of (1764), 38, 41

CABINET MISSION, 74
Calcutta, 28, 40, 50, 51, 58; foundation of, 38; captured by Nawab of Bengal, 38; Hindu-Muslim riots in, 75; refugee migration to, 93-4, 132; communism in, 125; International Communist Conference held in, 125; population, 179
Calicut, 39
Canada, 57
Carnatic, Nawab of the, 38, 40
Caste system: in Epic Age, 14; Hindu concept of, 17, 18; division of original four castes, 18-19; impact of Muslim Invasion, 26; in Kerala, 129; caste councils abolish formal excommunication, 153-4; decline of, 154-5
Catherine of Braganza, 38
Cattle, 172
Cavendish-Bentinck, Lord William. (*See* Bentinck)
Cave temples, 25
Cawnpore, 49
CENTO, 206
Central Asia, invaders from, 21, 23
Central Government Research Institute, 119
Central Parliament, 58; composition and jurisdiction of, 104; and the Untouchables, 107; party representation in, 124, 127, 128, 133, 135
Ceylon, 176; relations with India, 210
Chalukyas, 25
Chamar caste of Untouchables, 146-7
Chandernagore, 40
Chandigarh, 92
Chandragupta, Maurya, 21

Charles II, 38
Chembur, Atomic Energy Reactor at, 9
Chemical industry, 175
Chemistry, in ancient India, 22
Cherrapunji, 7
Chiang Kai-Shek, 206
Child sacrifice, made illegal, 44
China, 11, 20, 121, 122, 124, 126, 192, 207, 208, 210-11, 214, *96, 97*
Chittarajan, 180
Christianity, Christians, 16, 17, 132-3; in Kerala, 129, 130, 133
Churchill, Winston, 62, 70
Classification of Castes and Tribes, 55
Climate, 7
Clive, Robert (*See* Who's Who, p. 222), 40-1, *28*
Colour prejudice, 47-8, 205
Commonwealth, the, 209
Communications (radio, newspapers, etc.), 120-1
Communism, Nehru's opinion of, 89-90
Communist Party, Indian, 122, 124-7, 128, 206, *68*; wins majority in Kerala, 124-5, 130
Community Projects Extension, 158
Congress Party, 64, 70, 126-8, 192, 208; divided over question of violence, 56-7; success in 1937 elections, 71; popularity in 1947, 92; a national movement, 121-2; extent of support for, 122; strength, 123-4; programme, 124; communists within, 125; and women, 149; and planning, 180, 181; and foreign policy, 206
Constitution of the Republic of India: Preamble, 102; comes into effect, 102-3; the Executive, 103-4; the Central Parliament, 104; and the Rule of Law, 104-5; the Judiciary, 105; a working democracy, 105-6; the Fundamental Rights, 106-7
Coorgis, 8
Cornwallis, Charles (*See* Who's Who, p. 222), 42
Cotton textile industry, 175, 178, *84*

228

Fulbright, Senator, 124
Fundamental Rights of the Constitution, 106

GAMA, VASCO DA (*See* Who's Who, p. 222), 39, *21*, *22*
Ganatantra Parishad party, 128
Gandhi, Mahatma (*See* Who's Who, p. 222), 19, 50, 51, 55, 57, 61, 97, 106, 122, 125, 127, 153-5, 208, *36*, *37*, *38*, *40*; early life, and his beliefs, 61-6; and the Untouchables, 63, 65, 91, 107, 145; opposes British rule, 66-7; first imprisonment, 67-9; and the Round Table Conferences, 70; resigns from Congress Party, 70; rejects Cripps' offer, and launches 'Quit India' movement, 73, *42*; his half-fast, 75, *93*; preaches Hindu-Muslim brotherliness, 79-80, *39*; assassinated, 80; and Nehru, 89-90; and the language problem, 98, 100-1; on propaganda, 133; on the emancipation of women, 148, 149
Gangetic Valley, 24, 49, 50
García Lorca, Federico, *Yerma*, 194
Gladstone, W. E., 50
Goa, 39, 210
God, Hindu concept of, 15, 17, 18
Gokhale, G. K., 57, 62, 154
Golconda, conquered by Aurangzeb, 28
Goldwater, Senator, 124
Grand Trunk Road, 47
Grow More Food Campaign, 101
Gujerat, 8, 12, 67, 155; Swatantra Party in, 128; Anavil Brahmins of, 154
Gujerati language, 99
Gupta dynasty, 22
Gurkhas, 50

HAIR STYLES, 9
Halebid, temple of, 25
Handloom cloth, 175
Hanuman (monkey god), 15, 18
Harijans (official name for Untouchables), 147

Harsha period, 22
Hastings, Warren (*See* Who's Who, p. 222), 41-2, *29*
Hawkins, Captain William (*See* Who's Who, p. 223), 39
Health, 176, 193, *82*
Himalayas, 7, 8
Hindi: adopted as official language, 98-100; as third language in secondary education, 118; in universities, 119; in broadcasting, 120
Hindu Code, 148
Hindu-Mahasabha party, 122
Hindu-Muslim tension, 52, 58, 72, 75; after Partition, 92-4, 131-2
Hinduism, 9, 10, 23; based on the three great Epics, 14-16; its elastic philosophy, 17-18; its priesthood, 17, 150-1; rebels against, 19-21; impact of Muslim Invasion on, 26; and the status of women, 148
Hindus, 14; preoccupied with relationship between man and the divine, 12; religious duties of, 16-18; concept of God, 17; lack interest in history, 24; Moghul persecution of, 26, 28; improvement of education, 52; despised by Curzon, 56; treatment of in Pakistan, and their flight, 93, 94, 125, 132, 207; dislike drastic measures, 106; shift away from orthodoxy, 150; decline of caste amongst, 154
Hindustani, 98
Hirakud dam, 184, *88*
Hiuen-Tsang (Chinese traveller), 12
Hospitals, 176
Hume, A. O., 55
Hungary, 206, 211
Huns, 22
Hyderabad, Nizam of, 37, 38, 40, 78
Hyderabad State, 101, 125
Hygiene, 193

ICS. (*See* Indian Civil Service)
Iliad, 13-15

230

Madhya Pradesh become Buddhists,
134; government help for, 135; within
and without Hinduism, and their
groupings, 135; seats reserved for, in
Parliament, 135, 155; treatment of, in
villages, 145-7; and land reforms,
158

Upanishads, 14

Uralis of Kerala, 135

Urbanization: effect on joint-family
system, 152-3

Urdu language, 26

Uttar Pradesh, 38, 128, 131; and the
official language question, 98; literacy
rate, 117; Untouchables of, 146-7; hill-
Brahmins of, 154

Vedas, 13, 19

Vedic Age, 13

Viceroy's Legislative Council, 58, 59

Victoria, Queen, 39, 50, 57

Vijayanagar Empire, 27

Villages: diversity of, 8, 118, 52, 76;
treatment of Untouchables in, 145-7,
77; self-government for, and social
changes in, 158-9; population of, 169;

most of them cut off from markets, 185;
family life in, 194

Violence, organized, 126

Vishnu, 17, 18

Vokaligas (Brahmin subcaste), 135

WARRIORS CASTE, 48

Water supply, 173-4, *79, 80*

Wellesley, 1st Marquis, 38, 42-3

Wellington, Duke of, 38, 42

West Bengal, 56; refugee problem in,
93-4; riots in, 94; communism in, 125,
216; Hindu-Muslim tension in, 132

Wheat, 169

Widows, status of under the Rajputs, 233
(*See also* Suttee)

Witchcraft, 18

Women: and Hinduism, 18, 148; under
the Rajputs, 23; legal emancipation of,
80, 148-9; Gandhi's attitude to, 148,
149; effect of education on their
emancipation, 148-9

World Bank, 208; its Aid India Club,
177, 190

Zemindars (Indian tax-farmers), 42, 156

Zoroastrians, 134